Market Economics

Market Economics

Graham Walker

2nd Edition

TUDOR

Published by Tudor Educational
an imprint of
Liverpool Academic Press

First published in Great Britain in 2002 by Tudor Educational

© 2002 Graham Walker. 2nd Edition

ISBN 1-872807 84 4

British Library Cataloguing in Publication Data
A catalogue record for this book is available from the British Library

Typeset by Bitter & Twisted, N. Wales. Email: bitter@cybase.co.uk

Printed and Bound in Great Britain by
Lightning Source UK Ltd. Milton Keynes.

contents

preface & introduction

Market Economics provides a basic step by step approach to the theory and application of market analysis, in both micro and macro economics. The book explains, in a progressive manner, market analysis techniques and uses real world data case studies and multiple choice questions to illustrate. It covers both micro and macro analysis as follows: basic ideas, market analysis, market structures, cost behaviour and aggragate demand and supply. The book's comprehensive range of applications and assessment tests means it provides the tutor with an essential classroom tool as well as enabling the student to use the book as a revision aid.

The book will be essential for the new modular A/AS Curriculum 2000 Economics course. College students studying economics as a non-core subject will also find it useful as will those doing business, management and professional studies.

acknowledgements

The author would like to thank the following who have kindly given permission to use the published material as listed: CSO and the *Economist* etc. The author also thanks London University School Exam Board for permission to use 'A' level exam questions. Lastly I would like to thank Giles who has helped to design, type and illustrate this book. Any mistakes are my own.

G. Walker. 2002.

chapter one

Basic Economic Concepts

Aims

To define, explain and discuss

- The Method of Economics
- Economic Systems: Free Enterprise and Command
- Problems of Economics: What ? How ? Who ?
- Private and Public Goods: the Role of the Government

Key Concepts

Positive/Normative Statements; Economic Man; Economic Models; Consumer; Perishable; Capital Goods; Free Enterprise; Collectivist; Mixed Economy; Private; Collective; Public Goods; Cost; Rivalry; Merit/Demerit Goods; Externalities

Economics and Methodology

J.M. Keynes described the value of studying economics in terms of the thought process or method it developed when analysing a problem. Today the view is that economics uses a scientific method in so far as it employs theories with predictions that can be tested by empirical evidence. If the evidence disproves or refutes these predictions a new theory has to be developed. This approach is referred to as positive economics to distinguish it from normative economics which uses value judgments. An example illustrates. A positive statement is: 'a lower tea price causes more tea to be bought', whilst a normative statement would be: 'tea should be subsidised in order to encourage tea drinking'. The former statement can be tested by statistical evidence whilst the latter is a matter of opinion.

What is the scientific method which characterises physics or chemistry and how far can it be said to exist in economics ? The theories of physics and chemistry can be tested under controlled laboratory conditions but economics is a social science concerned with predicting human behaviour in the market place. This means it is often difficult to hold conditions constant in the real world in order to test economic theories accurately. Human behaviour is sometimes irrational and it is often impossible to pin down the main factor at work in an economic situation since so many may be influencing events. Nevertheless, overall statistical (econometric) analysis can be useful in explaining trends to both government and business sectors. What are the elements of the economic method ? Economics constructs a simulation or abstraction of the real world in the form of an economic model or hypothesis which links the behavioural cause to the predicted effect using certain basic assumptions. In market analysis a most important assumption is the 'ceterus paribus' clause (meaning other things remain constant). This enables specified market influences to be held constant in order to concentrate on one specific influence, such as price. These assumptions may not always be realistic but they do enable the economist to deduce testable predictions and therefore they show a systematic method of reasoning. The other approach is the inductive method which builds up explanatory theories on the basis of observation. Economists seem to use both methods. When Giffen observed the behaviour of Irish peasants buying more bread even when bread prices rose, he formulated the inductive idea of a Giffen good. On the other hand the neoclassical theory of the firm which allegedly uses unrealistic assumptions about business behaviour has developed a more deductive theory with respect to business price, output and profit. A summary of the scientific method in economic research is shown in figure 1.1.

Fig. 1.1 The Stages of Scientific Method in Economics

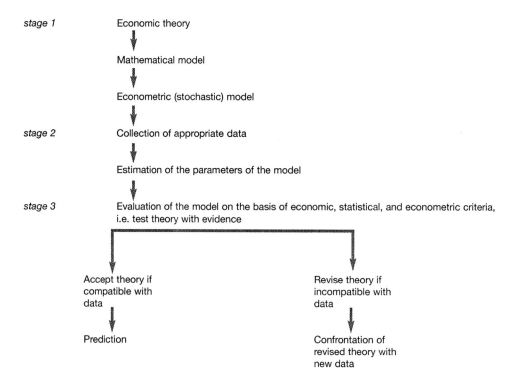

stage 1   Economic theory

                 Mathematical model

                 Econometric (stochastic) model

stage 2   Collection of appropriate data

                 Estimation of the parameters of the model

stage 3   Evaluation of the model on the basis of economic, statistical, and econometric criteria,
                 i.e. test theory with evidence

Accept theory if   Revise theory if
compatible with   incompatible with
data   data

Prediction   Confrontation of
                                              revised theory with
                                              new data

Economic Man and Arguments in Economics

Much of economics is concerned with decisions taken by the consumer, producer or income earner. In this it is assumed there is such a person as an economic man who, as an individual unit, is well-informed, rational and guided by material self-interest. Furthermore, this person makes unrestrained decisions based upon his own preferences for goals. These assumptions lie at the heart of much economic theory. However, in many areas of business, individuals behave in a social manner so that, it is alleged, people try to maximise the welfare of others before their own. Furthermore, uncertainty means that decisions are often non-scientific in nature and only recently has economics attempted to analyse economic behaviour under conditions of risk. The above helps to explain why economists often disagree. Economics is not an exact science and even simple definitions are open to argument. The classification of the unemployed has changed many times over the last few years. There are many disagreements about how realistic assumptions should be and also whether people are really guided by social or individualistic motives. Lastly, economists are bound to have their own political viewpoint which will colour their views on economic policy. Much of economics is concerned with inconclusive evidence so there is bound to be argument over policy decisions.

Micro and Macro Economics

Modern treatment divides the subject into micro and macro economics. Micro economics is concerned with the behaviour of the individual decision maker as well as a specific market and institutional operation. This is the subject matter of this book. Macro economics is concerned with overall problems affecting the economy such as inflation, unemployment, growth, etc.

The Economic System: Defining Economics

A selection of definitions of economics:

'A study of mankind in the ordinary business of life' *(Marshall)*.

'A study of human behaviour as a relationship between ends and scarce means which have alternative uses' *(Robbins)*.

'That part of human behaviour which relates to the production, exchange, and use of goods and services' *(Begg)*.

'The study of how people and society choose to employ scarce resources that could have alternative uses' *(Samuelson)*.

The central theme of the above definitions is that economics is concerned with the study of human behaviour with respect to resource allocation and use. Economic problems arise because there are limited resources but unlimited wants. This scarcity of resources means that a choice has to be made about what to produce. Human wants should not be confused with needs. Individuals have basic needs such as the need for shelter, clothing and food, and these needs, in a developed economy, are often the first to be provided. However, people are not satisfied with fulfilling these basic needs, they also want other goods and services which satisfy their yearning for social status and prestige, such as positional goods. Thus new wants, both individual and social in nature, are always developing and they are fulfilled by producers using scarce resources such as land, labour, capital and enterprise. These are also called factors of production and they are owned by the same individuals supplying the initial wants. The connection between wants and resources is made by the producer who brings together, in the business organisation, the factors in order to produce goods and services. These goods and services provide the satisfaction or utility to the consumer.

Economic goods and services have a scarcity value and can be classified as follows. Consumer perishables are consumed or used up immediately, (food, newspapers, etc) Consumer durables provide utility or satisfaction over a longer time period, (TV, motor car, video, etc) Personal services provide utility directly to the consumer (hair cuts, entertainment, holidays, etc) Commercial services help the individual obtain these goods by providing credit, insurance or retailing or wholesaling outlet, etc. Capital goods, also called producer or intermediate goods, provide utility indirectly by making the consumer goods used in final consumption. These capital goods are used by householders, companies and the state in the form of houses, motor cars, plant and equipment, factories, roads, hospitals, schools, etc. This means that a motor car is a consumer durable to an individual but to a company it could be classified as a fixed capital asset, that is helping indirectly in the production of final goods. When there is an abundance of a good, for example fresh air or sand in the desert, there will be no scarcity value and these are defined as free goods.

In producing the goods and services the producer in western economies combines factors of production in the best way (lowest cost) in order to achieve the objective of profit. Military, religious or other objectives can be pursued by other political systems. Nevertheless the problem of scarcity always exists. In some parts of Africa this scarcity is extreme and poverty exists, whilst in affluent western economies choice of scarcity is between one or two holidays a year. The universal economic problem of scarcity can be subdivided into the following areas:

- What goods and services are to be produced with the available resources?
- How are these resources best used in order to produce these goods and services?
- Who will receive these goods and services once they have been produced?

Two subsidiary problems associated with the above are:

- Where will production take place?
- When will production take place ?

Different economic systems have evolved to allocate scarce resources ranging from the free market to the command or collectivist system. The mixed economy lies between the extreme systems.

The Free Market System

The free market or free enterprise system is prevalent in the USA, Japan, the UK and other western democracies and generally exhibits the following features:

Individual Capital or Property

Individuals are allowed to own wealth in the form of land, houses and shares. Also they own their own companies, etc.

Free Enterprise Depends Upon Individual Self-Interest

Individuals can freely choose to consume or produce what they wish, guided by the motives of maximising satisfaction or profit. Individual factors of production will also seek the highest income.

Competition Within the Market

Competition is the overriding condition which affects both the consumer and the producer. Competition between buyers and sellers takes place within the market and this establishes the price for goods, services and factors of production (income). Ideally competition through the market serves to ensure prices are the correct signals to the consumer and producer and this information limits the powers of seller and buyer and automatically regulates the system.

Prices and Profit

The information for decision making comes from the prices and profits which arise in both product and factor markets. In order to ensure this market system works properly, consumers, producers and income earners must know how prices and profits change so that they can then adapt their buying and selling patterns to these price changes.

An example, using figure 1.2, serves to illustrate how the above features work in order to answer the scarcity problems outlined. The computer market is taken as the example, showing how the free enterprise system reacts to a sudden increase in the demand for computers by consumers.

Fig. 1.2 The Free Enterprise System - More Computers

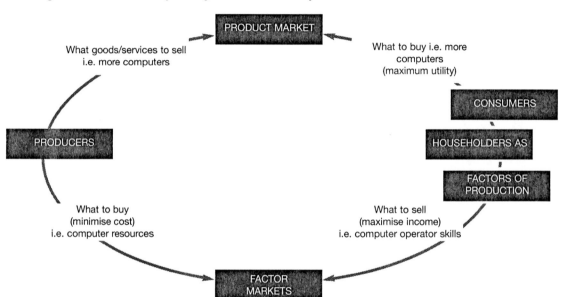

The computer product market will experience a rise in price and profits and producers may decide to move resources into making more computers at the expense of other goods which now make relatively lower profits, or even losses. The producers now hire more factors of production from factor markets and this will push up incomes to those in the computer factor market. Householders who ultimately own resources will now be attracted into the higher paid occupations in the computer sector. Furthermore, since they now earn high incomes, they will also have a greater claim over the goods and services produced. Capital, land resources, and entrepreneurial skills will all move to produce more computers so their incomes will also increase. Thus the free enterprise unit (sole trader, partnership or limited company) motivated by self-interest (profit) and guided by the market will help to solve the problem of (i) what to produce? - more computers; (ii) how to produce? -lowest cost, highest profit; and (iii) for whom? - those owning scarce computer resources who now earn higher incomes.

In order to make the right decisions, both producers and consumers will compare the extra benefits or revenues against the extra costs or risks before taking any action to make extra products or before moving their resources into a particular factor market. The above computer example also serves to illustrate the advantages of the free enterprise system.

The Advantages of the Free Market System

- Goods and services are produced in line with free consumer choice and wants.
- The price signals automatically and quickly inform consumers, producers and income earners how the market is changing.
- Competition encourages the lowest price for both product and factor markets so resources are quickly and efficiently used and not wasted.

Even so there are disadvantages of the free market system.

The Disadvantages of the Free Market System

- Inequalities of income and wealth will develop so that some may enjoy the luxuries of life before others have been properly fed or clothed.
- If competition does not exist due to monopolistic markets, then inefficiency and excessive profits can result.
- Consumers are not always able to make a fully-informed choice so resources may be used inefficiently.
- Important goods such as defence, law and order, health or education may not be provided in sufficient quantity through the market to guarantee a caring, civilised society.

The Command or Collectivist System

In this system, the state owns the resources, the means of production and by essential planning decides what to produce, how production is to take place and, by controlling factor incomes, how the output of the economy is to be distributed. Under this system, prices are set by the state, ('fiat' prices) and not by the market and hence the needs of the state are put above the individual wants of the consumer.

The Advantages of the Collectivist System

- In theory, basic needs can be provided for all before individual wants or luxuries are catered for.
- Social costs and benefits can be identified and valued so that resources can be allocated to improve the environment, or to reduce monopoly power or to provide adequate health services, etc.
- By owning the means of production, the state ensures continuous production of essentials and so helps to reduce the problems of unemployed resources which often result with the free market system.

Disadvantages of the Collectivist System

- In practice food shortages arise and consumer wants are usually ignored.
- There is a lack of incentive to provide goods because there is no profit motive and furthermore costs are often allowed to escalate because of a lack of accountability.
- Bureaucratic self-interest replaces the profit motive, waste increases and coordinating production decisions are often made difficult due to the absence of price signals and profits.
- Inequality of incomes does not disappear. The bureaucratic and state officials become the high income earners rather than the entrepreneurs.

The Mixed Economy

In this system, illustrated by the economies of the UK, Sweden, France, etc., the private entrepreneur and the state coexist to produce goods and services the consumer wants and needs. In the UK the private sector produces around 70 per cent of output with the state providing the rest. The state has a variety of roles.

Public and Merit Goods

Public goods, such as defence, roads, road signs, are provided by taxation because it is alleged that otherwise they would not be provided in sufficient quantity if left to the market. Merit goods, such as education and health, are those which the state provides because they are thought to be good for the community. These are discussed in more detail below.

Industrial Policy

The state has always attempted to regulate both factor and product markets. Factor markets, wage controls and trade union legislation have sought to achieve social and economic objectives. In product markets price controls and anti-monopolistic legislation have a long history in the UK The nationalisation of certain key industries, for example electricity, gas, coal, rail, was pursued after the second world war. Since the 1979 Thatcher Government, the role of the state in this area has been subject to critical review, and policy has been designed to privatise nationalised industries, encourage private provision in health and education and generally deregulate the controlled sectors.

Macroeconomic Management and Objectives (See Chapter 9)

After the second world war Keynesian demand management policies were used to reduce unemployment and generate economic growth, although since the 1980s a monetarist stance has been assumed which relies upon free market sources determining levels of inflation and unemployment. Generally the role of the state has reduced over the last few years and has now to be seen in the context of the state's aim to achieve greater economic and social equality against the free enterprise search for profit and efficiency.

Classification of Public, Collective and Private Goods

In order to understand the state versus free enterprise argument it is useful to classify the types of goods and services provided in a mixed economy. The matrix in table 1.1 identifies four groups of goods according to the criteria of rivalry and excludability.

Table 1.1 Private, Collective and Public Goods

	Rivalrous or Positive Cost in Consumption	Non-Rivalrous or Costless in Consumption
Excludable from Non-Payer	Private Goods e.g. Cars, Food	Toll Goods e.g. Bridges, Roads
Not Excludable from Non-Payer	Common Goods e.g. Fishing	Public Goods e.g. Road Signs, Defence, Fireworks, Lighthouse

Rivalrous

Rivalry in consumption means that if one person consumes a good then that good cannot be consumed by another: it has a positive opportunity cost. If it is non-rivalrous in consumption then the enjoyment of the good by one person does not prevent other people from consuming and enjoying the same good: one person's use of a bridge, under normal circumstances, would not stop another person using it at the same time.

In fact the use of road signs by others provides positive benefits to everyone.

Excludable

Excludability means it is possible to provide the good on a one to one basis, for example one person uses one pair of shoes. Thus a non-excludable good is one where it is not possible to exclude others from consuming even if they have not paid, for example a private fireworks function which is overlooked by others. From the table private goods are those which are both excludable and rivalrous whilst the other three categories are generally classified as collective goods since they either are non-excludable, non-rivalrous or both. In these three cases of goods which are called collective goods the state often finances, by taxation, the operation and provision of the goods or services.

Merit/Demerit Goods

Merit goods, such as health and education, are thought by the state to be good for the community, so their consumption is actively encouraged by free state provision or some sort of subsidy. Demerit goods, such as smoking, alcohol, drugs, etc., are not thought by the state to be good for the individual so the production and consumption of these goods is discouraged by taxation or other regulations.

Externalities and Social Costs

External social benefits and costs are those extra costs and benefits that fall outside the market decision by either buyer or seller. They are ignored because the market only values benefits and costs to the buyer and private seller. These external benefits and costs are nevertheless enjoyed or borne by the community. External social costs would be the extra pollution or congestion which society has to pay for, whilst social benefits would be the fruits of a healthy and well-educated society. It is alleged that the free market ignores these costs and benefits so the state has to play a role ensuring that they are appreciated.

Positional Goods

They are an extreme form of private good: very exclusive and wanted because they afford social status. Only a few can obtain or afford them, e.g. membership of a club. They indicate standing or position in society. Positional goods are characterised by an inelastic supply and increasing demand.

Opportunity Costs and Diminishing Returns

As wants are unlimited and resources limited, there has to be a choice between goods consumed and hence goods produced. This choice implies that a good will be given up, foregone, when another is chosen. This is true concept of opportunity cost, and it shows the cost of consumption (guns or butter) in production (wheat or barley) and even when governments chose between schools rather than hospitals. We can usefully illustrate both the problem of scarcity and choice, of which the conflict between current consumption and capital formation is a prime example, by the use of production possibility curves (PPC) which show opportunity costs.

In order to illustrate this concept we will assume that our economy is capable of producing two goods, good X and good Y. It has the choice of devoting all its resources to the production of good X and having none of good Y, devoting all its resources to good Y and having none of good X, or choosing some intermediate point and having some of both. This is illustrated in figure 1.3. At point C some of both are produced. Note that the shape of the PPC is concave to the origin; this is because we move along the curve from A toward B and factors of production are transferred from the production of one good to the other. As successive units of the factors of production are transferred they will be less and less efficient in their new use due to diminishing returns, and for each of unit of Y sacrificed we will gain smaller and smaller quantities of X, i.e. the opportunity cost increases. This illustrates that in an economy which is fully utilising its resources substitution is inevitable and wherever there are scarce resources society must always make choices. At point U society's resources are under-utilised and we can have more of both goods by moving on to the PPC. Point Z is unobtainable and can only be achieved by a shift of the whole curve upwards and outwards; this can only occur as a result of technological change, increased productivity or an increase in available resources.

Fig. 1.3

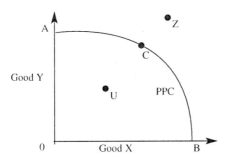

Figure 1.4 illustrates a society which has chosen in the current time period (t) a high

level of consumer goods and a lower level of capital goods.

Fig. 1.4

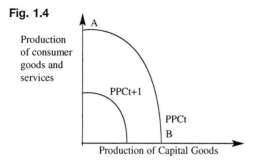

In the next time period (t+1) the PPC has shifted towards the origin to PPCt+1 producing less of both goods and therefore a lower standard of living. Figure 1.5 illustrates a society which in the current time period has chosen to have a high level of production of capital goods and a relatively lower level of production of consumer goods for current consumption. In the next time period (t+1) however, the PPC has shifted outwards to PPCt+1, and society enjoys a higher level of consumption and capital formation.

Fig. 1.5

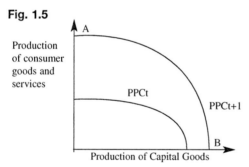

Diminishing Returns

It cannot be assumed however that because we have more of a factor available we can always gain proportionate increases in output, as inevitably the returns from additional units of factors of production will tend to decline. This is referred to as the law of diminishing returns or declining marginal productivity. This states that as we add additional units of a variable factor to a constant factor then the product (output) of the variable factor will first of all rise but will eventually start to decline.

The theory assumes that all the units of the variable factor are identical in terms of productivity, and the techniques of production remain unchanged. In table 1.2 total product refers to the total output of the variable factor, in this case labour. Marginal product refers to the increase in total product from each additional unit of labour and

average product = $\dfrac{\text{total product}}{\text{quantity of labour}}$

In table 1.2 we illustrate the example of a smallholder with one acre of land growing potatoes employing at first a single unit of labour then employing more and more labourers and keeping the amount of land constant. This is represented graphically in figure 1.6.

During the first phase as additional labour is added to the fixed factor (land) each successive unit raises output and total product (TP), marginal product (MP) and average product (AP) are all rising. This continues until the fifth man is added when MP reaches a peak and falls sharply cutting AP at its highest point after which AP also declines. During the second phase, after the addition of the fifth unit of labour, the rate of growth of TP declines and both AP and MP decline, MP declining more sharply than AP. Up to the fifth man total product increases at an increasing rate and there are increasing returns. After the fifth man the rate of growth of total product declines and diminishing returns set in as the marginal product declines. In the third phase at the point where total product beings to fall, after the ninth man, marginal product becomes negative. The diminishing marginal product of labour underpins the demand for labour (see Chapter 4).

Table 1.2

Labour	Total Product (Tonnes)	Average Product (AP)	Marginal Product (MP)
1	2	2	
2	10	5	8
3	21	7	11
4	36	9	15
5	55	11	19
6	63	10.5	8
7	70	10	7
8	72	9	2
9	72	8	0

Fig. 1.6

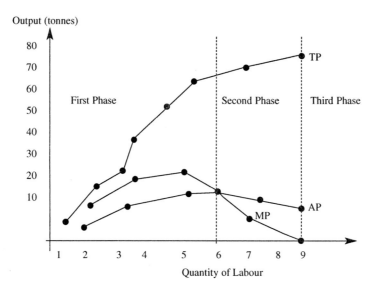

Specialisation and Trade

Originally primitive societies were only able to produce enough output for self-sufficiency or autarky. This meant little or no excess output was available to trade and so individuals were prevented from specialising in what they were good at doing, e.g. hunting for fishing, since they had to do everything for themselves. Therefore societies were unable to exploit their natural resources. These resources could have taken the form of an abundance of land, mineral wealth or an ability to farm the land, etc. The development of free political democratic societies, money, and free enterprise systems, enabled individuals and regions to concentrate on producing and then trading those goods where costs were lowest. This enabled them to exploit their natural resources and also meant that others could, by trade, enjoy these advantages. Industries developed which were able to concentrate on producing a narrow range of products efficiently and, in the simplest form, led to the breaking down of complex tasks into simple repetitive jobs, i.e. division of labour. Adam Smith quotes the famous pin factory example where the making of one pin is broken down into 18 different operations. The output of the pin factory was far higher per head by this process of specialisation than would have been the case if one man had produced the whole pin. The specialisation process eventually led to a variety of craft and professional occupations as well as specialisation firms and industries and a concentration of specialist production facilities in regions and countries. Mass production technologies were developed to exploit this and, by this standardisation of components and products, efficiency increased further. Specialisation led to excess production and hence trade, which increases overall output, income and economic welfare. At the simplest level, individuals perform a specialist task for an income which they then trade for the goods and services they are no longer able to produce. This is also the basis for trade between countries. Advantages from trade and specialisation are illustrated by absolute and comparative advantage as outlined by David Ricardo. Examples are as follows.

Example One - Absolute Advantage

Suppose two people, A and B, are able to produce wine and cheese. A takes one hour of labour to produce one pound of cheese and two hours of labour to produce one gallon of wine. B, on the other hand, takes two hours and one hour to produce one pound of cheese and one gallon of wine respectively. This means that A has an absolute advantage in producing cheese and B has an absolute advantage in producing wine because each is able to produce these products using less labour than the other. If they were to specialise in what they are best or more efficient at producing, they could then trade any surplus and still end up better off than under self-sufficiency. Table 1.3 shows the matrices (i) self-sufficiency and (ii) after trade, to illustrate. Exchange is on the basis of one gallon of wine for one pound of cheese, i.e. these rates are the terms of trade of cheese for wine.

Table 1.3

(i) **Hours required to make**			(ii) **Hours required after trade**		
	1 lb Cheese	1 gall Wine		1 lb Cheese	1 gall Wine
A	1	2	A	1	1
B	2	1	B	1	1

Note: Terms of Trade 1.1

A can specialise in cheese and sell one pound of cheese for one gallon of wine, i.e. the opportunity cost now of one pound of cheese is now one gallon of wine, whereas before, to produce one pound of cheese meant that he had to give us two pounds of cheese. The same applies to B with respect to cheese for wine. Their effort now enables them to obtain more of the product they had to work two hours each for.

Example Two - Comparative Advantage

Even if A were more efficient in time of hours worked in producing both wine and cheese, it would still pay A as an individual or as a country to specialise and trade.

Suppose now it takes A one hour of labour to make a pound of cheese and two hours of labour to make a gallon of wine. In B it takes six hours to make a pound of cheese and three hours to make a gallon of wine, i.e. A is more efficient in both goods but is more so in cheese. If the price or terms of trade is still one to one, then it is still worthwhile specialising and then trading. In A, more efficient in making both goods, an hour of labour can produce one unit of cheese or half a unit of wine. However, as 1lb of cheese can be traded for one gallon of wine, it makes sense for A to specialise in cheese and trade some cheese for wine. So A can consume as much cheese as before but twice as much wine. B is less efficient than A in producing both wine and cheese. An hour of B's labour can make 1/6th of a pound of cheese and 1/3rd of a gallon of wine; which is worth 1/3rd of a 1lb of cheese in the market. so B can specialise in wine and trades wine for cheese. This means that B can consume as much wine as before and twice as much cheese. These situations are shown in matrices (i) and (ii) in table 1.4.

Table 1.4

(i) **Before specialisation** hours required to make			(ii) **Hours required after trade**		
	1 lb Cheese	1 gall Wine		1 lb Cheese	1 gall Wine
A	1	2	A	1	1
B	6	3	B	3	3

Note: Terms of Trade 1.1

In this case B, through trade, has an opportunity to produce at lowest cost the good in which it has a comparative advantage. This analysis explains why both individuals and countries specialise and trade. However, the above does assume that both A and B are perfectly able to move between producing wine or cheese (there is perfect mobility). Also, it assumes that there is a constancy in terms of hours required to produce more of each good, i.e. constant returns. Finally, the terms of trade of wine for cheese are always mutually beneficial. In the real world these conditions may not always apply, e.g. cheese or wine can be heavily taxed so A or B might find themselves once more better off producing their own wine or cheese.

The Advantages of Specialisation

- Specialisation enables mass production and hence mass consumption of those goods in which individuals and countries have absolute and comparative advantage.
- Specialisation leads to uniform and identical products and components which are interchangeable and universally recognised and purchased.
- Specialisation enables labour, land and capital to improve productivity as they

become more task specific. This improves individual skills and talents, and allows capital to become specialised which reduces costs and releases resources for use elsewhere.

■ Specialisation enables consumers to benefit from the natural advantages of their neighbours in terms of lower cost products, i.e. economic welfare and efficiency increased.

The Disadvantages of Specialisation

■ Specialisation leads factors of production and countries to over-dependence upon a particular task or product which is exported. If demand for a product is hit in a slump, then the factors of production will be unemployment and the country will be badly affected.

■ Specialisation can lead to capital, labour and land becoming too job specific and so unadaptable to a change in demand.

■ Specialisation leads to increasing interdependence between industries, occupations and countries which may suffer if any one part or link in the chain breaks down.

Protectionism (see page 51)

Specialisation leads to free trade between regions of countries but hindrances in the form of quotas, tariffs, currency controls and quality controls are often imposed to limit free trade, ie. protectionism, in order to:-

a. protect new infant industries against low price world imports in order to develop long term economies of scale

b. protect national security ie. we should not import from enemies

c. protect jobs and industries from low cost subsidised imports ie. dumping

d. limit the damage to our balance of payments and deter others from protectionism.

Organisation/Main Types

Table 1.5 identifies the main forms of commercial organisation in the UK together with their main business features and characteristics.

Table 1.5   Organisations: Main Types

Type of business (Legal Forms)	No involved in owner-ship	Examples	Success of finance (Major)	Who is liable for debts	Profit to	Authority and control of Business
Sole Proprietor	1	Hairdresser Plumber	Bank loans & or personal savings, HP finance, credit	Owner is fully liable for all debts incurred	Owner keeps all profits	Full control of proprietor
Partnership	2-20	Doctors, solicitors dentists surveyors	Bank loans &/or personal savings, HP, finance mortgages etc	At least one partner is fully liable for all debts	Profits shared according to deed of partnership	All partners have equal power (except sleeping partners) see 1907 Act
Private joint stock company	2 or more	Small local builder	All of the above the issue of shares to agreed members	Limited liability for debts. Each shareholder only risks the amount put in to buy shares	Distributed between all shareholders - dividends being paid per share	Normally directed by shareholders (in proportion to the number of shares held)
Public joint -stock company	2 or more	ICI, Shell Sainsburys Marks & Spencer	All of the above but ownership of shares is open to all via the stock exchange eg public issue	As for private joint stock company. But annual general report must be available to the public and accounts publicised in the national press. (A minimum amount of share capital is another prerequisite)		Shareholders appoint a board or directors to act on their behalf (These directors are voted in/out at the AGM)

Note:

(1) all the above types of business organisations are owned and controlled by private individuals, that is, they form part of the private sector. In contrast government-funded and organised firms (not detailed above) constitute the public sector e.g. British Rail.

(2) Since the 1980 Companies Act, a private joint-stock company must include the word "limited" in its title, and a public joint-stock company must have the words "public limited company" at the end of its name e.g. Marks & Spencers plc.

Sole Proprietor

This is the form of business unit used by a single individual, for example a plumber, who provides the capital, runs the business himself, and takes all the risks and hence the profit. There are drawbacks to being a sole proprietor. The major one is unlimited liability for the owner in the event of financial problems. This means that an individual can lose all personal assets in settlement of the debt. The sole proprietor bears all the risk, runs the business without the help of a partner and is often hampered by lack of finance.

Partnerships

There are two main types:

- Ordinary Partnerships as set up by Partnership Act of 1890 and,
- Limited Partnership as controlled by the Limited Partnership Act of 1907.

The latter form of partnership is unusual since the benefit of limited liability can be obtained as a private company. A limited partnership arises when a partner, i.e. a sleeping partner, invests in a business but takes no part in the operation or management. In ordinary partnerships all partners take part in the management and running of the business and as such all partners are jointly and severally liable for any debts incurred by the partnership. The usual advantage of this partnership type is that more than one person shares in the decision-making so each person can specialise in different management functions. On the other hand there are disadvantages. If one partner disagrees with the others and leaves, the partnership must be dissolved. Partnerships generally suffer a lack of adequate finance and furthermore the partnership cannot sue or be sued in its own name but only in the name of a partner or partners. Also, a partner can act as a representative of the business and bind his fellow partners in a contract. Finally, a partner may not transfer his shares of the business without consent of fellow partners.

Private and Public Joint Stock Companies

Joint stock companies exist as a separate legal entity from the shareholders who own the business, so the business can sue or be sued. These bodies are also known as corporations. Joint stock companies are able to raise capital by issuing ordinary shares which, by the end of the 19th century, carried the privilege of limited liability for shareholders. This means that shareholders cannot loose any more money than the nominal share issue or stock in which they have invested. These corporations grow by take-overs and are now referred to as conglomerates and multinationals. As well as being a separate legal entity a company is unaffected by a change of membership to the board of directors or shareholders, i.e. there is continuity.

The main differences between a private and a public company are as follows:

- a private company, unlike a public company, cannot trade its shares on the Stock Exchange,
- a private company cannot sell shares and debentures to the public, unlike a public company,
- shares of a public company are freely transferable whereas the shareholder of a private company has first to obtain the other members permission to trade shares,

- a private company trades once it has registered whereas a public company must also have a Trading Certificate.

However, both public and private companies are regulated by:

- Memorandum of Association which sets out the company objectives, types of business operation and its legal identity.
- The Articles of Association which outline the internal rules of the company, the powers, rights and obligations of its members etc.
- The Companies Act 1985 which set out for private and public companies the legal framework for running and liquidating a company.

The above regulations mean there can be a difference between those who own business (shareholders) and those who manage (board of directors).

Business Units - Size and Growth

Measurement of Scale

Concentration Ratios (CRs)

A typical concentration ratio is the five firm industry ratio which indicates how much output or market share the five largest firms, or business units, in the industry produce when compared to the whole industry's output. This is given by the formula

$$CR5 = \frac{\text{output of largest five firms}}{\text{output of whole industry}} \times \frac{100}{1}$$

In manufacturing industries such as brewing, cement, motor car production, etc., the CR5 would be around 60 - 70% concentration.

Minimum Scale of Efficiency (MSE)

This defines the output level where the firms average cost becomes horizontal. This output level also identifies efficient levels of production and in UK manufacturing the MSE for any one organisation would be represent significant shares in the market for cigarettes, refrigerators, petrol refining.

Turnover or Capital Assets Employed

This is a simple measure to identify the largest companies in an economy or an industry in terms of sales turnover or capital assets employed.

Methods of Growth

Business units become large by:

- Internal growth, i.e. by building new plants or outlets from internal profit, or share issues, e.g. Marks and Spencers.
- Mergers; more usual is the process where two firms agree to merge by setting up a holding company.
- Takeover; where one firm buys up one or more other firms.

Reasons for Mergers and Takeovers

- To exploit economies of scale. This normally requires the complete reorganisation of all economic operations and is usually concentrated on particular economies, e.g. market economies, etc.
- To dominate the market, i.e. this is where the growth in the size of the business is used to exploit monopoly power in particular industrial sectors.
- To stabilise the market share of the business unit, or secure its sources of supply in terms of inputs and often to maintain its output.
- Diversification; by buying up different businesses involved in a variety of consumer or industrial markets, the business is able to spread its risk. Increasingly this is the main reason to day for conglomerates business growth.
- Asset stripping. When a company's asset value is greater than its share price, then the acquirer can sell off the most valuable assets of a company in order to make capital gains.

Types of Integration

There are three types of integration: horizontal, vertical and lateral. Each of these is illustrated in table 1.6 which uses brewing and leisure as examples.

Table 1.6

Stage of Production	Brewing Units		Leisure (fast foods)	
i. Tertiary (Pubs/outlets)	X X	X	X (Restaurants, Hotels etc.)
ii. Manufacturer (Brewery)	X X			
iii. Extractive (Hop farms)	X X			

Table 1.6 shows initially six separate and independent business units in the brewing sector and two units in the leisure sector. This situation then changes by the following processes.

Horizontal Integration

If the two brewers amalgamated at the same stage of production, this is referred to as horizontal integration and would include the amalgamation of the pubs and/or the hop farms. The motives for horizontal integration are: to gain economies of scale in marketing, to reduce competition or to gain control of the market by building up monopoly power. Currently around 70% of all mergers are horizontal.

Vertical - (forward/backward)

Vertical integration is when a business unit takes over a producer in the same industry but at a different stage of production. Forward vertical integration would include the brewers who take over the marketing outlets (pubs) at the tertiary or service stage of production. This is usually done in order to control the market price of the good or to control the distribution network and hence diversify into other retail sectors. Vertical backwards integration is when the brewers then proceed to take over the sources of their input supplies, e.g. hop farms. This form of integration is usually undertaken in order to control input prices, to ensure the certainty and continuity of good quality inputs and also to diversify into other market areas. Vertical integration accounts for 5% of all mergers.

Lateral Integration

This is the creation of conglomerates or holding companies. In this case the conglomerate buys into business units which are unrelated to each other and to the original industries. Thus the brewers may buy into the leisure industry, e.g. fast food chains or health farms, etc. This is done in order to exploit managerial economies of scale and also to diversify and spread risk across a number of markets. One method of doing this financially is by using a holding or parent company which has a significant shareholding in other companies and can control their activities. Lateral integration is now commonplace in the UK, e.g. Hanson Trust, BAT, Whitbread Trust, etc. This form of integration accounts for 25% of all mergers. Sears Holdings Ltd, for example, has interests in cutlery production, shipbuilding, footwear, engineering, department stores and insurance. In view of the pressures which lead to business units growing in scale, it is important to appreciate that the small scale firm still plays an important role in the UK industrial structure.

The Survival of the Small Firm

Definition of a Small Firm

The Bolton Committee which investigated the small firm in the UK suggested a variety of measures for defining a small business unit including sales turnover, number of employees, share of the total market, etc. None of these criteria provided an overall, realistic or consistent definition. The 1981 Companies Act defined a small firm as one with up to 50 employees, less than £700,000 worth of assets or with a sales turnover up to £1.4m per annum.

Main Areas of Activity

Despite the increase in the scale of production, illustrated by growing concentration ratios, small scale units still dominate in market areas such as road haulage, the motor trade, restaurants and catering, retailing, building and hotel business. The reasons for the survival of the small firm are as follows.

Small Market Size

When demand is small scale, personalised, irregular, or seasonal in nature, then neither the product nor the service can be standardised. This means mass production methods and economies of scale cannot be exploited. This concept is illustrated by Adam Smith's maxim that 'specialisation is limited by the extent of the market'.

Personalised or Bespoke Service

When personal attention and service is required a large unit would not be able to provide this individualistic service, e.g. personal tailor.

The Business Owner

Often the owner of the business does not wish to increase the size of the firm, rather preferring to remain in control. In retailing, by binding together in a co-operative organisation, e.g. Spar, smallscale retailers are able to buy in bulk. Furthermore, this type of operator can also maintain the goodwill of the customers.

Stage of Growth

The smallness of the business may be because the firm is at an early stage of industrial growth. It may in due course become a large firm.

Flexibility and Risk Aversion

In the building industry the small contractor works for a major sub-contractor and this provides flexibility for both firms. The main sub-contractor finds that this arrangement reduces his financial risk because he is no longer responsible for employing a large work force. This reduces the problems of man management and, because of the uncertainty factor with respect to future work, it reduces the risk of heavy investment in machinery which would then lead to the growth of scale.

The Political Climate

The Conservative economic philosophy of the 1980s in the UK encouraged the growth of small, self-employed unit by using a variety of tax concessions and other financial incentives. However, in times of recession, bankruptcy is highest among this group.

The Location of the Industry

Location economics seeks to explain where production takes place, whether the business unit is small- or large-scale, involved in primary, manufacturing or tertiary industry, whether it is private enterprise or a government agency. Overall economic forces usually dictate where the unit locates.

Micro-economic Factors

Generally, the profit-maximising entrepreneur will seek to locate in order to maximise profit or minimise costs and maximise revenue.

Raw Materials

Heavy industries locate where low-cost raw material supplies are available and these attract other associated industries, e.g. steel and shipbuilding were attracted to coal fields in the north.

Transport

The maintenance of low transport costs was the main factor influencing location in the UK in the 19th century. Most heavy industries tended to locate near cheap sources of transport, e.g. rivers or canals. These days the availability of good and efficient transport facilities such as roads or railways is still a major consideration. Weber analysed transport costs as the prime location factor and classified goods into those with low and high value to weight ratios. Those with low value to weight ratios would locate close to the raw material source whilst those with high value to weight ratios, e.g. consumer goods, would locate near the market. In the case of the latter type of goods industries have now become footloose with respect to material costs and will often be influenced by the availability of labour.

Labour

Modern location economics emphasises that cheap labour is not as important as availability of skilled labour. For most high-tech industries the spread of automation in both factory and office has reduced the need for unskilled labour.

Power

Originally industries such as wool and cotton manufacturing were located near cheap sources of power but with the supply of electricity and the national grid system, many engineering firms can now locate in any region they choose, i.e. they are footloose.

External Economies

Many industries and business units congregate where other associated and complementary industries are established. This is done in order to exploit economies of scale which improves efficiency and lowers unit costs. External economies are such things as the nearness to associated markets, a trained and available work force, good communications, improved road or rail links. This explains why financial institutions gravitate towards the centre of London and why mechanical engineering firms move to the Midlands.

Market Influences

The growth of consumer goods industries providing personal goods and services has meant that businesses tend to locate close to the market. For example, catering, retailing, education, health services, entertainment and professional services, are all to be found within major centres of population. In the London area there are many consumer goods industries attracted by the magnet of high incomes.

Social Factors

A major new factor affecting the businessman is environmental or social influence. This takes the form of cheap housing, an attractive countryside and other social factors.

Economic Behaviour - Risk and Uncertainty

Economic decisions are often taken under conditions of risk and uncertainty, both in product and factor markets. Whereas risk can be statistically assessed and allowed for, uncertainty is impossible to predict and, because of this, markets may not be able to work efficiently. Uncertainty and risk arise under the following circumstances.

- Unforeseen demand and supply changes in agricultural markets can lead to wide variations in price and income especially when demand and supply are inelastic.(See Chapter 3).

- Ordinary share price movements are highly volatile and many change because of non-economic factors. Random price movements are recognised and have been reported. These are often unpredicted and inexplicable.

- Accidents such as fires, etc., can wipe out business stocks and profits overnight. Personal accidents affecting the workforce can also require expensive medical attention.

- Investment decisions can incorrectly predict future costs, revenues, profits and interest rates. This is more likely to happen the further the project is planned into the future.

- Current tender prices have to include and calculate future costs of materials which have yet to be produced or purchased.

Businessmen and consumers are regarded by economists as risk averse. This means that people would prefer not to take on a fair bet, i.e. one with a 50/50 chance of winning, because the extra utility of a wealthy gain is less than the extra utility of a wealth loss. This is especially true as the scale of the loss or gain increases. Thus both the individuals and businessmen look for ways of reducing risk often by buying an insurance policy which offsets it. In the case of insurance, some have estimated that the premium is in fact around 30% more than the statistical probability of the event occurring. At the same time, with respect to the above example of a 50/50 bet, those who are indifferent about taking on the bet are said to be risk neutral, whilst those keen on the bet are classified as risk lovers.

Methods and Markets to Offset Risk

The Insurance Method

This is a long-established technique for reducing financial risk whereby individuals, for a premium, pay insurance companies to take over the risk on those events which can be statistically assessed. Although this puts up the fixed costs of a business it allows the business to provide for a larger, more certain scale of activity and hence tends to encourage competition. This means the number of potential competitors in an industry is increased, leading to more efficiency.

Speculators

These operate in financial, commodity agricultural markets. Their role is to buy when prices are low and to sell in order to make a profit when prices are high. This has the effect of stabilising price and so encourages these markets to operate and develop products and services which otherwise would not be produced.

Forward Traders

In both commodity and financial markets forward traders provide the certainty of a predetermined forward price which reduces the risk to the businessman. It allows businessmen to hedge against unforeseen risk and so encourages these markets to operate and develop products and services which otherwise would not be produced.

Portfolio Analysis

This is a new technique of analysis by which overall risk is reduced in equity and investment markets. Essentially it leads to analysis investing in a broad range of shares. Some shares tend to move with the market, some against the market and some in an erratic, unpredicted fashion. By not putting all the financial eggs in one basket, this type of analysis encourages trade and hence investment in traders financial assets. Associated techniques such as probability and sensitivity analysis attempt to isolate the key significant variables most likely to affect the outcome in order that a measured and informed investment decision can be taken.

Market Research and Good Management Practices

Professional management attempts to reduce risk by thorough research of both product and factor markets. Before recruiting or launching new products, intensive research will be undertaken. Nevertheless there are two major problems in this: adverse selection and moral hazard.

Adverse Selection and Moral Hazard in Risk Markets

In insurance markets adverse selection means that high risk, i.e., high cost clients are more likely to take out insurance than the low or medium risk clients on whom the premiums have been assessed. In labour markets adverse selection means that those who apply for jobs are often the ones least suitable. However, the cost of reducing the business risk in the insurance market and the cost of correcting selection procedures in the labour market may lead to such a high price that the consumer is unable to afford it. One way of overcoming this is by sophisticated recruitment procedures in the labour market and by a system of weighting bad risk clients in the insurance market. Moral hazard refers to the concept whereby the insured policy holder may behave in such a way as to increase the likelihood of the undesired outcome actually occurring. This, in the case of car insurance, may lead to poor driving which increases accident claims and makes premiums expensive. Some even claim that seatbelts increase the likelihood of motor car accidents because the driver has less to fear by driving fast. These two problems can increase uncertainty and the cost of insurance. Moral hazard is a problem with respect to unemployment insurance because it can affect people's attitude to work. It may reduce the willingness to look for a job because the individual may be able to claim unemployment benefit too easily. In health markets where national insurance applies only an irrational person would behave in such a way as to claim medical insurance by having an accident in order to occupy a hospital bed.

Business Decisions- a General Overview

A business has to make a variety of decisions in order to produce the most profitable output using its resources. In this it has to decide the product, the quantity and quality of the product and also how to locate and how best to raise the capital it uses for the technology it employs. In selling the product the business, subject to market structure, has to decide upon the channels of distribution, advertising policy and the best mixture of home and overseas markets. A business unit can take on a number of different forms, e.g. a partnership, sole trader, or joint stock company and a decision will have to be made as to the most suitable type of business unit. It has also to determine a policy with respect to the government which will impose a variety of regulations in produce and factor markets. Lastly a business has to decide upon the degree of acceptable risk and how best to reduce uncertainty in the markets. The following analysis in both product and factor markets assumes zero risk of uncertainty unless otherwise stated.

Data Response 1 Basic Concepts

Social Influences on Expenditure

The range of private consumption that contains a social element in the sense described is much wider than is generally recognised. In textbooks on economics public goods are discussed in the context of goods and facilities that can be provided only, or most economically, on a collective basis, open to all and financed by all. City parks and streets and national defence are prominent examples. In addition, elements of public goods are recognised in side effects of private transactions such as pollution and congestion occurring in particular identifiable situations. But a more general public goods element can be attributed to a wide range of private expenditures. Thus the utility of expenditure on a given level of education as a means of access to the most sought-after jobs will decline as more people attain that level of education. The value to me of my education depends not only on how much I have but also on how much the man ahead of me in the job line has. The satisfaction derived from an auto or a country cottage (positional goods) depends on the conditions in which they can be used, which will be strongly influenced by how many other people are using them. This factor, which is social in origin, may be a more important influence on my satisfaction than the characteristics of these items as 'private' goods (on the speed of the auto, the spaciousness of the cottage, and so forth).

Source: F. Hirsch, *Social Limits of Growth*, Routledge and Kegan Paul, 1977

1. Outline the difference between social and private expenditure, as referred to in economics textbooks. Give examples of both kinds of expenditure, according to this definition.

2. How does the writer use the example of education to show how the traditional distinction between social and private expenditure breaks down?

3. How do you see the crucial difference between 'positional goods' such as education and country cottages, and goods such as cans of baked beans?

Data Response 2

Comparative Economic Statistics

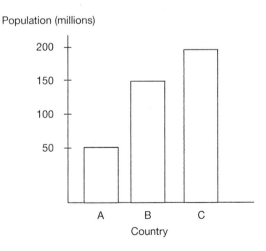

Population (millions) / Country

Land area, population and GNP in three different countries (A, B, C)

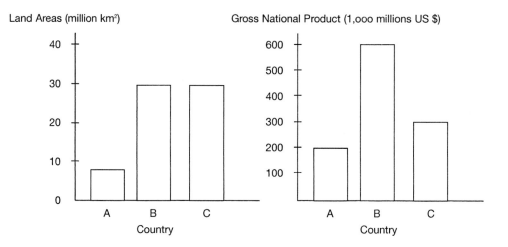

Land Areas (million km²)

Gross National Product (1,000 millions US $)

Questions

1. Calculate per capita income for each country and comment on your findings.

2. Comment upon variations in factor endowments between countries A, B and C.

3. Using your findings in Q1, discuss the idea of optimum population viz. B and C.

Data Response 3

Five Policies for Growth in Eastern Europe

With hindsight it is clear that to work, reform needs to include five main elements.

1. Financial Reform

An unchecked flow of finance to loss-making enterprises undermines incentives to control costs or achieve greater efficiency. It also creates further difficulties that, in the West, would be organised under three separate headings: fiscal policy, monetary control and banking supervision.

First, such subsidies are a form of public spending over which the government is exercising no control. (As a rule, East European countries did not count flows of money to loss-making enterprises as public spending their true budget deficits were much bigger than their reported ones). Second, because the subsidies are supplied directly by the central bank, they fuel an inflationary expansion of the money supply. Third, where state-run banks have acted as intermediaries, enterprises have run up debts to them that will prove unpayable.

To deal with all this, reformers need to impose financial discipline on enterprises. That will require curbing or halting the flow of credit. They need to introduce proper methods of fiscal control, and to finance public spending mainly, out of taxes. And they need to create a commercial banking system that cares about its own profitability.

2. Institution-building

The ex-communist economies lack the institutions of capitalism. These include: systems of law to regulate contracts forms of corporate ownership, bankruptcy and so forth; tax systems that are based on rules and formulas rather than arbitrary retention of income by the state; privately owned banks and other financial intermediaries: settled conventions of accounting and book-keeping.

3. Price Reform

In a market economy, prices move to balance supply and demand. They are the signals that direct resources to their most efficient uses. When prices are freed, scarce goods become more expensive - but that is the incentive for more production.

4. Privatisation

A lesson of the partial reforms of the 1960s was that giving managers and workers greater freedom to run their enterprises had a drawback. Because the assets of the enterprise were owned by the state, managers had no reason to maintain their value. They often chose instead to invest less and pay bigger wages. Under capitalism, the private owner of productive assets holds the company's managers accountable.

Many East-European enterprises, also, were monopolies or near-monopolies. If resources are to be used efficiently, these need to be broken up and the parts allowed to compete against each other. Privatisation is the likeliest way to achieve this.

5. Trade reform

To open their economies fully, governments have to dismantle trade barriers and make their currencies convertible for trade. Free trade does two things. First, it forces enterprises to compete with foreign suppliers. Introducing competition in to the domestic economy, by breaking up firms and privatising them, takes time, through trade in the West, the power of competition can be harnessed quickly. Second, openness to trade forces domestic prices into line with world prices, ensuring that the signals which guide the use of resources are not distorted.

The extract 'Five policies for growth in Eastern Europe' outlines five methods intended to stimulate economic growth in the ex-communist countries of Eastern Europe.

1. Write a summary of each policy in your own words.

2. Outline the long-term benefits of each policy.

3. Analyse the short-term costs of each policy and suggest who would be likely to bear these costs.

Data Response 4
Comparative Advantages

Specialisation

Country A and B can produce the following output with given labour units

Hours needed to produce

	1 car	1 computer
Country A	10	20
Country B	50	30

1. Identify the country which has absolute and comparative advantage in cars and computers.

2. Which country will specialise in cars and which in computers?

3. If the terms of trade are one car to one computer, then the gain to A will be the equivalent of, (i) one extra car or (ii) two extra computers, after trade?

4. If B exports computers for cars the gain to B for each car imported is the equivalent of (i) a cost saving of 66.33% (ii) one extra car (iii) 30 hours saved (iv) none of these?

5. If the terms of trade are now one car to two computers then B is now (i) worse off than when self sufficient (ii) as well as before (iii) still better off by 20%.

Multiple Choice

1. Which of the following statements is *normative*?

    a. The free market allocates resources via the price system

    b. Rationing essential goods ensures that all consumers can obtain some of these goods

    c. In a centralised economy resources are allocated by government directive

    d. Queuing is an unfair method of allocating resources

    e. Rationing and queuing are indicative of shortages of supply

    f. None of these.

2. Non-excludability and non-rivalry are characteristics of:

   a. private goods

   b. merit goods

   c. public goods

   d. inferior goods

   e. normal goods

   f. positional goods.

3. The opportunity cost of a factor of production is best defined as:

   a. the amount a firm must pay out currently to secure the use of that particular factor

   b. the cost that was met when the factor was originally purchased

   c. the extra cost involved when one more unit is purchased

   d. the cost of replacing one unit of the factor

   e. the value of the next best use of that factor

   f.   none of these.

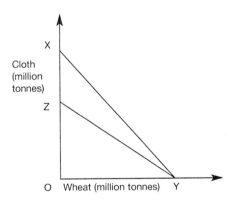

4. The diagram above refers to an economy producing only two commodities, cloth and wheat. Initially, the economy has production possibilities as shown by the line XY. The production possibility line then moves to ZY. This change could be caused by:

   a. a decrease in the demand for cloth

   b. unemployment in the cloth industry

   c. an increase in the demand for wheat

   d. a rise in the costs of producing cloth in terms of wheat

e. a fall in the cost of raw materials for cloth manufacture

f. none of these.

g. What do lines XY, ZY say about opportunity costs?

5. Which of the following situations illustrate moral hazard and which adverse selection?

    a. Fred never locks his car, knowing it is insured for theft.

    b. George takes out life insurance, knowing that his work in mining has given him terminal lung cancer.

    c. George takes out extra health insurance before going on a mountaineering holiday.

    d. 'Those who can't, teach and those who can't teach administer'.

6. Tom, Dick and Harry are each offered the opportunity of buying a second-hand car for £1,000. However, there is a 50:50 chance that the car's real value is double that. Tom refuses the deal, Dick decides by tossing a coin and Harry is keen to buy.

How would you describe each person's attitude to risk. Match the person to the characteristics.

    a. Tom   (i)   Risk averse

    b. Dick   (ii)   Risk neutral

    c. Harry   (iii) Risk lover

7. Eric wishes to invest £100 in shares. Two industries, petrol and retailing, have shares on offer at £50 each. The returns from each are independent and in each case there is a 50% chance that returns will be good (£20) and a 50% chance that returns will be poor (£5).

    a. If Eric buys petrol shares and times are (i) good (ii) bad, what will be the return each case and on average?

    b. If Eric buys retail shares and times are (i) good (ii) bad, what will be the return in each case and on average?

    c. If you put your money into just one industry, what is the chance of a poor return.

    d. What is the average return if Eric diversifies?.

    e. If Eric diversifies, compare the likelihood of a poor return compared to the likelihood of a poor return by not diversifying.

chapter two

How Price is Determined

Aims

To define, explain and discuss

- Markets and Functions
- Price Determination
- Application and Evaluation of Market Analysis

Key Concepts

Demand; Supply; Equilibrium Price; Substitutes; Complements; Income; Expectations; Price Controls; Perverse Demand; Buffer Stocks; Market Failure; Product Factor Goods; Market Links

A market is a set of institutional arrangements which allows buyers and sellers to exchange goods and services for some agreed price.

Basic Characteristics of Product/Factor Markets

- Markets are local, national and/or international in nature. They can exist in one place or be geographically dispersed and connected by telephone, etc. Markets exist in many forms, such as auctions, ring trading or most usually as a private contract, for example the second-hand car market.
- Markets are regular or irregular in their frequency and exist for products, factors of production, personal or financial services, etc. They can be for a flow of new goods or for a stock of existing goods and assets.

- Markets range from those which are free and competitive to those dominated by the monopolistic buyer or seller. Within this range market structures can be oligopolistic with a few players, duopolistic with two producers or they can be competitively monopolistic which means there can be many producers selling a slightly different product, each having a small market share.

- Most markets are, to some extent, influenced and possibly distorted by government intervention which takes a variety of forms such as price controls, rules and regulations, taxation and subsidies. In many cases the government may be the only buyer or seller. The reason for government intervention is because markets do not always operate efficiently, quickly or smoothly and so governments try to improve the overall performance of markets.

- Markets operate currently so the forces of supply and demand determine the day's spot price, or they can be used to determine future prices for commodities and currencies. Futures markets reduce uncertainty. Expectations play an important part in markets. Buyers and sellers adapt their behaviour about future prices based upon how prices have behaved in the past and how they expect prices to behave in the future. Many prices quoted in today's markets are based upon not only today's market forces but what is expected to happen to future demand and supply.

- Markets determine the price of a good, which is not the same as its value to an individual or a society. Price is the result of a demand for scarce resources in a market interacting with its supply, whilst value is a subjective view which includes the idea of need. The concept of value is difficult to analyse because political and psychological factors influence how the value of a good is perceived. Market analysis is concerned with price in terms of how much can be afforded with respect to the supply in the market.

- In the real world prices behave in a variety of ways. Price can fluctuate wildly, remain stable or be subject to slight increases or decreases over time. Market analysis sets out to build a simplified model of how market forces work, in terms of demand and supply, in order to explain and predict future movements in the market.

Demand as a Market Force

The market model of demand refers to effective demand which is the quantity of a good which will be demanded or bought at any given price over some time period, where it is backed up by a consumer's purchasing power. In the example, (see Fig. 2.1) market demand is the result of the addition of individual demand for the product, for example widgets, at different prices. The behaviour of the individual demand schedule is discussed later (see section on individual demand) The initial assumptions about market demand are:

- The price of widgets is the only variable changing and other factors such as income, etc. are given (ceterus paribus applies).
- The price is the real price so inflation does not exist.
- The rational consumer behaves consistently so the shape of the demand schedule reflects both an income and substitution effect. If the price of the good falls then real income or purchasing power of the consumer rises. This means if the price falls the consumer will buy more, that is substitute in favour of the relatively cheap good. Also because income rises even more of the good will be bought. In this case the good is a normal good and the income and substitution effect work to increase the amount of the good purchased; the opposite will apply if the price of the good falls.
- Individuals behave as if they were independent agents in determining their buying decisions, so demand is competitive and does not reflect collusion or monopolistic agreements.

Fig. 2.1 Individual and Market Demand for Widgets

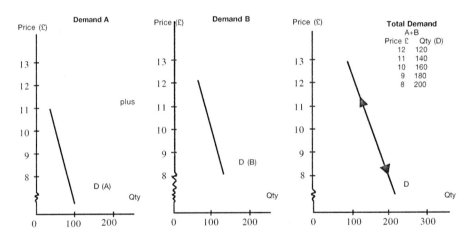

Determining the Market Demand for Widgets

Figure 2.1 shows how, by adding together A and B's demand for widgets, total demand is arrived at and this shows how much product is demanded at each price. As price falls more widgets are bought and vice versa as price rises. Demand contracts as price rises and expands as price falls, so there is an inverse relationship between demand and price.

The Perverse Demand Curve/Income and Substitution Effects

The law of demand says that the price of the good and the quantity demanded are usually inversely related. However, there are circumstances when demand curves slope upwards. In order to understand clearly why and how these examples occur, it is important to be clear about price (substitution) and income effects and how they combine to affect the demand curve. Figure 2.2 column (a) show four demand schedules. Demand curves (i), (ii) are schedules where more is bought as price falls, whilst schedules (iii) and (iv) are perverse as they slope upwards with respect to price. Column (b) shows how demand changes relate to income changes. A normal response is where more is bought when income rises whilst an abnormal or inferior response is the opposite with respect to income. There are four possibilities when price and income effects are combined with respect to quantity demanded. Situation (i) is the orthodox or normal case, i.e. income and substitution effects work in the same director to increase demand when price falls. Situation (ii) shows a case where there is a positive substitution effect which outweighs a negative (inferior) income effect. So overall demand still slopes downwards, e.g. an inferior good such as bread still exhibits overall a downward sloping demand schedule with respect to price. Situation (iii) shows where a negative income effect outweighs a positive substitution effect so overall demand slopes upwards, e.g. the Giffen Good case. Finally, situation (iv) shows where the positive income effect is outweighed by a negative substitution effect so more utility is gained as the price rises, i.e. people want goods of ostentation because of their social appeal. This last case also explains why speculators, who expect prices to rise even more, buy shares even when their prices are increasing. Furthermore, when quality is perceived to be indicative of the price, consumers will often buy more as the price rises because they may feel they are getting a better product. Demand is thus upward sloping with respect to price.

Fig. 2.2 Normal & Perverse Demand

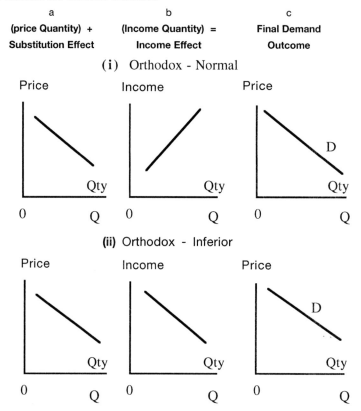

a	b	c
(price Quantity) +	(Income Quantity) =	Final Demand
Substitution Effect	Income Effect	Outcome

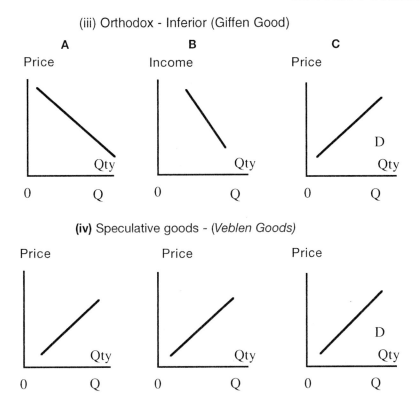

(iii) Orthodox - Inferior (Giffen Good)

A
Price

B
Income

C
Price

D

Qty

Qty

Qty

0   Q   0   Q   0   Q

(iv) Speculative goods - (Veblen Goods)

Price

Price

Price

D

Qty

Qty

Qty

0   Q   0   Q   0   Q

Determining the Market Supply for Widgets

The supply and demand curves referred to are shown as straight lines in order to facilitate the explanations. The supply schedule (see fig. 2.3) and curve for widgets shows the relationship between market price and the quantity each competitive (independent) supplier will put onto the market. Supply is a flow concept and shows the amount the supplier produces for the market over a period of time at different prices. The simple supply schedule is illustrated in figure 2.3 and this illustrates the idea that more will be supplied at a high price and less at the low price, that is there is a direct relationship between price and the quantity supplied. The supply curve reflects rising marginal costs for individual suppliers A and B and hence for the industry, which is the combined output of all producers' supply schedules. Although factor input prices are constant, diminishing returns means that unit output costs rise so requiring a higher price in the market to offset these costs. Movements along the supply curve reflect an expansion of supply as price rises and a contraction of supply as price falls.

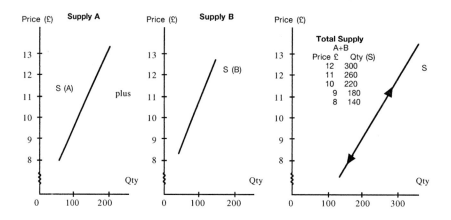

Fig. 2.3 Individual and Market Supply for Widgets

Supply and Demand and Market Price

If supply and demand for widgets are brought together, with respect to price, in the free market then there will only be one price where quantity demanded and supplied are equal. This is the equilibrium price in figure 2.4, at £9 and here demand and supply will be 180 units. If the price was temporarily at £8 then demand will exceed supply by 60 units and so there will be a shortage and price will be pushed up. If there were a temporary price of £10 in the market this would result in a surplus of 60 units so price would now be forced down. Thus market forces work to move the price to an equilibrium at £9 where there is stability.

Fig. 2.4 Market Equilibrium for Widgets

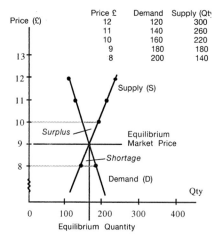

The Market for Perishables and Equilibrium Price

If the product has a short life, for example perishable goods, and suppliers supply a non-equilibrium quantity of 200 units at a price of £9.50 (see Fig. 2.5) then in order to clear the market the price will have to drop to £8. This price may appear to be the equilibrium price as well as the market price by suppliers. At this price, demand exceeds the supply by 60 units and now price will be bid up to £11 because at £8 demand is 200 and supply is 140. This means the market will become unstable because of the nature of the good. However, when the product can be gradually increased or decreased in production, the equilibrium will be slowly reached as in figure 2.4. Because perishable goods have a short shelf life, then there is a possibility of a non-stable market situation. This is also true when individual competitive suppliers are ignorant of all relevant supply and demand conditions.

Fig. 2.5 The Market for Perishable Goods

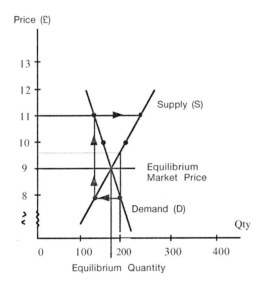

Demand for Widgets - Other Demand Factors

A change in demand can occur because factors, other than the price of the product (widgets), change and influence the consumer. At each price an extra 60 units will be demanded. Conversely, a fall in demand means 60 fewer widgets will be demanded at each price and the price of the good is assumed to remain constant, ceterus paribus. As figure 2.6 shows, these changes shift the whole demand schedule to the right (or the left) of the original demand.

Fig. 2.6 Demand Shifts and Impact upon Price

Price	Quality Demanded (D)	D1
12	120	180
11	140	200
10	160	220
9	180	240
8	200	260

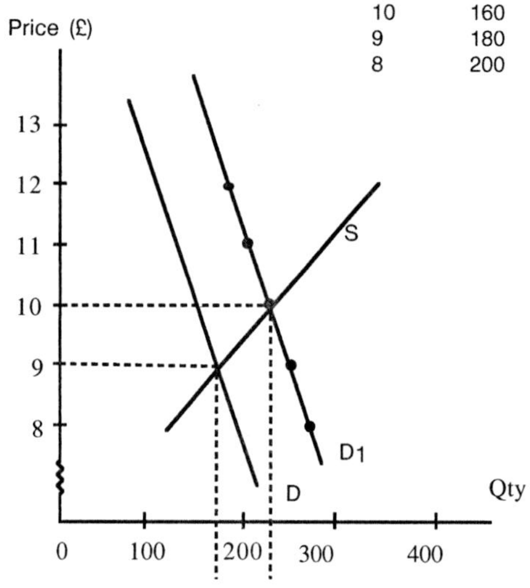

The main factors affecting demand are as follows.

Real Disposable Income (RDI)

This refers to the value of income, after adjusting for inflation, net of deductions for tax, etc. It is very important in influencing demand for expensive consumer durable goods, where income increases also increase the demand for the good, that is they are normal goods. However, in the case of inferior goods less are bought as income rises and in some cases only so much of a good can be consumed (satiation goods) regardless of income. If taxation policies change so high spending incomes are taxed more than before, then this new distribution of tax will lead to a fall in demand: it will shift demand to the left since disposable incomes have now fallen.

The Price of Related Goods

The two categories of related goods are substitutes and complementary goods. Substitute goods are alternatives for each other, for example coffee or tea, whilst complements are goods which are bought together, such as petrol and cars. This means if the price of tea falls we would expect consumers to buy more tea and less coffee and the demand for coffee would shift to the left. In the case of widgets, if 60 more are demanded, it would have been because the price of the substitute had risen. In the case of complements, a fall in the price of petrol would lead to a rise in demand, so demand shifts to the right. This relationship is also referred to as joint demand. In the case of house purchase and credit, these two products are purchased normally at the same time, so cheaper credit normally increases the demand for houses and shifts demand to the right.

Expectations

Increasingly consumers attempt to predict what will happen to the price of a good in the future. Thus if it is expected that the price of widgets will increase, perhaps due to some rise in tax on widgets, then demand today will increase by 60 units. Expectations are important in explaining price changes in financial markets where asset price changes give rise to capital gains.

Other Demand Factors

These factors cover such influences as taste, fashion and advertising which can all increase or decrease (shift) demand. This is true in consumer goods markets where taste has recently moved in favour of low fat goods. The size of the market is also important, for example more old people will increase demand for health services. Seasonal demand patterns explain why the demand for cards increases at Christmas.

The impact of a change (increase) in the demand for widgets upon market price is shown in figure 2.6. At the old price of £9 demand now exceeds supply by 60 units. This shortage leads to a rise in price to £10 where market price is in equilibrium with 220 units bought and sold. If demand decreases by 60 units at an original equilibrium market price of £10, then at this price supply now exceeds demand so there is a surplus which forces suppliers to reduce price to a new equilibrium of £9. Thus the initial increase in demand is 60 units, but after price changes the resultant increase is only 40 units: the old equilibrium quantity was 180 at £9 and the new equilibrium quantity is 220 units at the new price of £10.

Supply of Widgets - Other Supply Factors

Changes in supply occur when more or less is supplied at each price by suppliers. Alternatively for some output level, for example 200, the shift to S1 means in figure 2.7 suppliers are willing to accept a lower price of £8 than before. Factors which shift the supply curve are as follows (ceterus paribus).

Productivity Gains

If unit input costs fall or unit output, per factor input, rises then overall average unit costs will decrease across the whole industry and so suppliers will be willing to offer the same quantity at a lower price. These gains in productivity will be due to improvement in management, better machinery, improved labour productivity or better cost saving technology resulting from innovation or improved techniques. This shifts S to S1.

Fig. 2.7 Supply Changes (Shifts) and Price

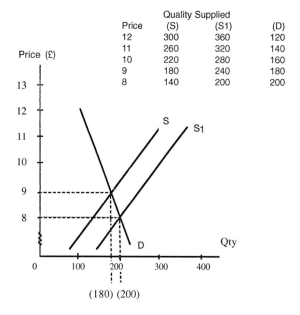

Price	Quality Supplied (S)	(S1)	(D)
12	300	360	120
11	260	320	140
10	220	280	160
9	180	240	180
8	140	200	200

Factor Cost Changes

If the unit cost of factor inputs, such as wages, rent, interest rates or materials, falls then even if productivity remains constant unit output costs, that is selling prices, will decline. However, if factor costs fall by the same amount as productivity declines, then supply remains constant. Factor costs can also reduce if cheaper substitute materials can be used, for example plastic rather than cast iron gutterings in the building industry.

Weather and Agricultural Yields

In many agricultural sectors the weather can have a considerable impact. A rainy spell can reduce the yield and even with the same factor inputs of fertiliser and manpower the supply will shift to the left, that is S1 to S.

Government Taxation and Subsidies

The imposition of an indirect tax, such as VAT, will shift the supply from S1 to S and this will have the same impact as a rise in costs or a fall in productivity. A reduction in VAT or a subsidy given to the producer, will shift supply from S to S1 and so act in the same way as a fall in cost.

The Impact of a Supply Shift on Market Price

As shown in figure 2.7, supply shifts from S to S1 with demand (D) shown. At the original price of £9 supply now exceeds demand for widgets by 60 units and so market forces push down the price to a new equilibrium of £8 where demand and supply quantity is 200 units. If supply had shifted from S1 to S, due to the fall in the productivity of the industry, the market price would have risen from £8 to £9.

Special Demand and Supply Relationships

The following indicate some applications for the above analysis regarding changes in the demand and supply conditions with respect to particular relationships.

Joint Demand/Complementary Goods

In the case of complementary goods such as petrol/cars (see figure 2.8) the change in the price of one will affect the demand for the other because they are jointly demanded. If petrol costs rise and price goes from 0p to 0p1, this reduces the overall demand for cars from D to D1 and the price of cars falls from 0p to 0p1.

Fig. 2.8 Joint Demand

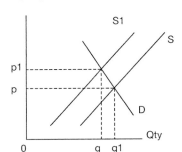

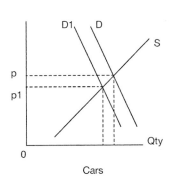

Competitive Demand/Substitutes

Products such as tea and coffee (see figure 2.9) could be viewed as substitutes and so the demand for one will vary directly with the price of its substitute. If a bad harvest reduces the supply of coffee from S to S1 and pushes up prices from 0p to 0p1,then demand for tea will increase from D to D1 as people substitute in favour of cheaper tea. This eventually pushes up tea prices from 0p to 0p1.

Fig. 2.9 Competitive Demand

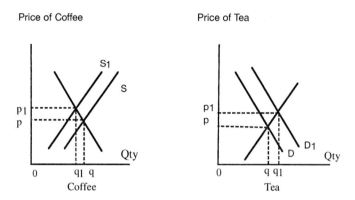

Composite Demand/Several Uses for the Same Good

Often there are several uses for the same good (see fig.2.10). Steel can be used to build cars or for construction purposes. If the demand for steel to build cars increases from D to D1 and pushes up steel prices, this will shift the supply schedule for construction steel from S to S1 and so push up construction prices. This reduces demand and quantity falls from 0q to 0q1.

Fig. 2.10 Composite Demand

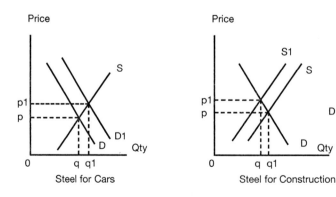

Joint Supply

This is where the production of one product, for example cows, automatically increases the supply of another, that is leather derived from cow (see fig. 2.11). Similarly in air transport an outward journey gives rise to an inward one. When demand for beef cattle rises from D to D1, cow production increases output from 0q to 0q1. This shifts the supply of leather goods from S to S1 and reduces price from 0p to 0p1.

Fig. 2.11 Joint Supply

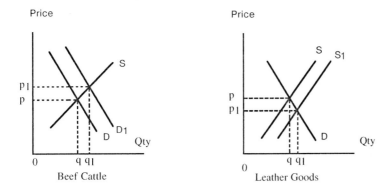

Market Changes Over Time

Although changes in demand shift demand in the short term very quickly, changes in supply, due to cost, etc., normally occur over a longer period. This means for a given change in demand from D to D1 price adjustments occur from the immediate to the medium and thence the long term. In the immediate term supply is often fixed at 0q so price rises from 0p1 to 0p4 as demand increases. In the medium term, output gradually increases, 0q to 0q2 as factors of production move into the industry, so price changes to 0p3. In the long term the industry is able to adjust fully to demand and supply shifts to S1 so the new long term price and output equilibrium is 0p2/0q3.

Fig. 2.12 Market Changes Over Time

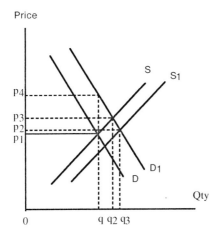

Applications of Market Analysis

Free and Controlled Prices

The petrol market exists under both a free market, for example the Rotterdam spot market, and a controlled petrol market price, such as OPEC. It could be argued that the free market price influences the cartel or control price, see figure 2.13. In this case lower non-OPEC oil prices push down world petrol prices from 0p1 to 0p and this forces OPEC to reduce its price from 0p1 to 0p.

Fig. 2.13 Controlled/Free Markets

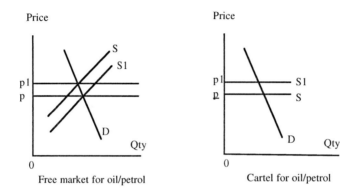

Market Failure: Unsatisfied Demand/Consumers Surplus

In the case of unsatisfied demand, that is market failure, there will be no price where consumers would be able to purchase because minimum supply price is always higher than the price consumers are prepared to buy, see figure 2.14 (a). This problem can be corrected by governments subsidising production, as in the case of cars for the disabled, or by allowing in cheap imports at a price where demand can exist. In the case of figure 2.14 (b) at a price of 0p there is still an unsatisfied demand of 0q2 - 0q. Cheap imports at 0p1 reduce unsatisfied demand to only 0q2 - 0q1 so consumer surplus has been gained by this lower price. A zero price maximises consumer surplus and means unsatisfied demand no longer exists. Consumer surplus occurs when people buy the good for less than they would be willing to pay.

Fig. 2.14 Market Failure and Unsatisfied Demand

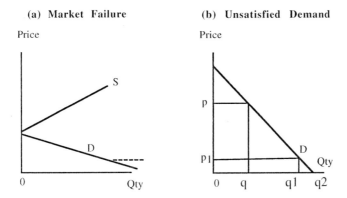

Demand for Money or Cash Balances

The demand for money arises because people need to pay their bills, have cash for emergency purposes or use money in order to speculate and make a profit. If they hold too little in their current account (cash balances) they may run the risk of having to borrow at even higher cost or pay excessive bank charges for being overdrawn. The demand curve for money/cash balances reflects these pressures (see fig.2.15) . Demand for money balances is inversely related to interest paid on money holdings. People will hold more cash at lower interest rates because the convenience factor outweighs the loss of interest, and it also enables people to quickly move their cash into profit making ventures, for example buying shares which rise in price. When interest rates are high cash holdings fall because the cost of cash for convenience purposes rises in terms of the higher interest paid for giving up cash balances.

Fig. 2.15 Demand for Money

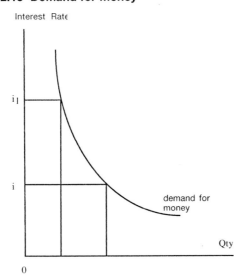

The Relationship Between Product and Factor Markets

Although market analysis has so far been applied to product markets, such as eggs and widgets, it also can be applied to factors of production such as land, labour and capital. Furthermore the impact of a change in the product market with respect to substitute products such as tea and coffee can be traced through factor markets; the supply and demand for labour in the tea and coffee plantations. Figure 2.16 illustrates these concepts. In the example, demand for tea increases whilst demand for coffee decreases. This pushes up tea prices and reduces coffee prices. Resources (labour) are moved into tea production as the demand for labour pushes up tea workers' wages and at the same time demand for coffee workers pushes down the wages of coffee labourers. The market mechanism operates in order to produce more of what is wanted by using more labour resources. As the wages of tea workers rise they have a greater claim on what is produced, that is the what, how and for whom questions of economics are illustrated in this example.

Fig. 2.16 The Relationship Between Product and Factor Markets

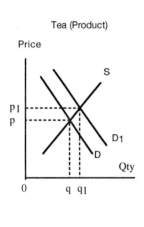

Tea (Product)

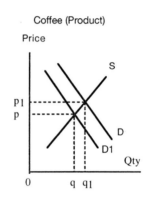

Coffee (Product)

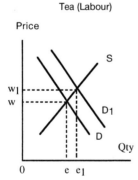

Tea (Labour)

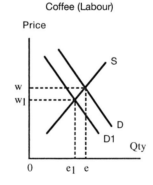

Coffee (Labour)

Applications of Market Analysis: International Trade and Markets

Countries trade because consumers can import products at a world market price (A + B), which is less than the home equilibrium price, and producers can export at a world price greater than the home price. Figure 2.17 illustrates, where country A imports and country B exports.

Free Trade Intervention

A tariff placed upon imports into A will raise the price (see line Y in A) and will reduce imports, hence reducing exports from B (see line Z). A quota to reduce imports into A (see line X in A) will push up the price above the home equilibrium price in A. The extra revenue generated by the tariff will go to the government and the quota will push up profits to importers.

Fig. 2.17 International Trade and Intervention

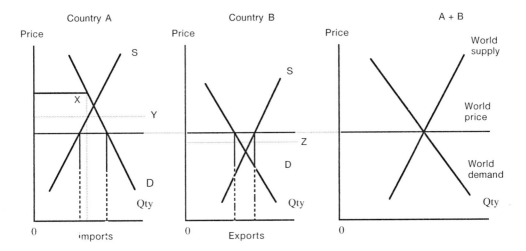

The Value of the Pound (See Fig 2.18)

The value of the pound, in terms of for example the US dollar, reflects demand for UK exports and the supply of US imports. Demand for pounds reflects the demand for UK exports of goods and services, while the supply of pounds reflects the derived demand of UK consumers for US goods and services. In equilibrium, the value of the pound at £1=$1.60 means that, theoretically, the value of UK imports and exports are the same and the balance of payments is in balance.

The Market for the Pound

If the pound was temporarily out of equilibrium at $2 or $1, then there would be a respective deficit and surplus on the balance of payments at these values (see fig 2.18).

Fig. 2.18 The Market for the Pound

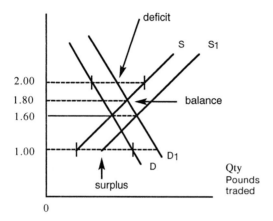

Changing the Value of the Pound

A shift in demand for pounds to D1 would initially mean there is a shortage of pounds at $1.60, which would disappear as the pound rises to $1.80 (see Fig. 2.18). This increase in demand for pounds could be because:

- Pounds were bought by speculators, attracted by UK interest rates, who then sell weaker currencies to obtain pounds.
- Government policy aimed at reducing inflation increasing competitiveness immediately moves the market to predict a stronger value for the pound.
- Overall world demand increases and British export goods become more popular.

Note: for some industries, an increasing value of the pound at $1.80 could make exporting less competitive. Even though the free market floating value of the pound is $1.80, the UK government may wish to fix the value at $1.60. This could be achieved through the selling of pounds by the government, S to S1. It could also occur if the government deliberately reduced UK interest rates to force the pound down.

Applications of Market Analysis: Intervention in Markets

Governments and Price Controls

Governments often wish to fix price above, or as in the case shown in figure 2.19 (i) below equilibrium price of 0p at 0p2. This may be in order to achieve some social objective such as ensuring all can afford to purchase the good. However, the consequences may be other than was anticipated. In the first place demand now exceeds supply at 0p2 by an amount 0q2 less 0q1. This excess demand may now become a problem in other markets. Supply reduces in this market and those lucky enough to obtain the goods do so at a price of 0p2. Left to the free market the limited supply of 0q1 may be forced up in price by a 'black market' to a price of 0p1 which is above the equilibrium which would have arisen in an unregulated market. If the government wish to allocate 0q1 it could do so by a variety of methods, such as rationing by using coupons, queuing or even by a system of bribery to those bureaucrats allocating 0q1. In the event of a queuing system, person A, (see Fig. 2.19 (ii)), obtains all they need of the scarce good by being first in the queue, that is 0q1, whilst person B is unable to purchase anything at all. However, person B values the first unit of the scarce good at a price of 0p1, whilst person A values the good at only 0p2. Thus trade between them would improve the situation until an overall level of 0p obtains for A and B. This result would have occurred if left to the free market. Also a control price of 0p1 in figure 2.19 (i) above the equilibrium, would have led to an excess supply of 0q2 less 0q1 which could also lead to expensive storage problems as well as a waste of these scarce resources.

Fig. 2.19 Governments and Price Controls

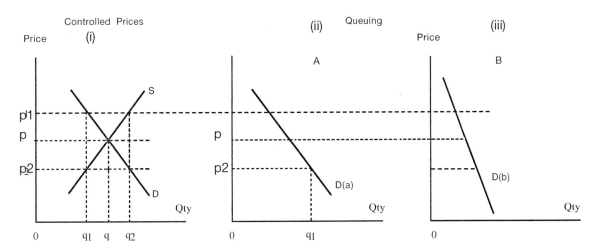

Buffer Stock Arrangements to Stabilise Agricultural Price Fluctuations

If the government wishes the price of eggs to be stabilised at 0p as in figure 2.20 (b) it would attempt to plan output of 0q so the revenue in the industry is equivalent to 0p x 0q. It may also realise that unplanned output can fluctuate between S1 and S2 which would lead to price fluctuations between 0p1 and p2. In order to stabilise price at 0p the government could operate a buffer stock system. This means it would buy up excess stock of 0q1 - 0q in order to push price from p1 to p and it would sell off this stock in the event of a shortage, 0q - 0q2, to stop the price rising to 0p2. However, if producers saw 0p as a guaranteed price they might be encouraged to permanently produce beyond 0q and so taxpayers' money is used to build up increasingly wasteful stocks.

Fig. 2.20 Buffer Stock Arrangements.

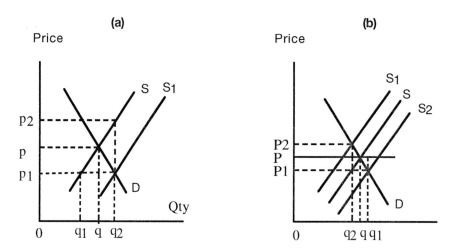

Quotas, Imports and Subsidies

In order to overcome the overproduction problem a quota system could be used so that each producer is allocated a quota proportional to 0q in figure 2.20 (b). However, this is criticised because it does not encourage the lowest cost producers to produce most because each is given the same output amount to produce. In some agricultural markets (see Fig. 2.20 (a)) world imports at a price of 0p1 may be allowed in the home market. This will lead to a home production level of 0q1 and an import level of 0q2 less 0q1. Home producers may also be paid a subsidy of 0p2 less 0p in order to support the home industry. This may lead in the long term to a supply shift from S to S1 which provides self-sufficiency at the world price. A tariff of 0p2 less 0p1 could also achieve this level of self-sufficiency but a high home price may not encourage long-term self-sufficiency levels. Again, if the government wish to stabilise price at 0p1, then when demand increases and threatens 0p1 the government could allow imports in. Imports are used as a buffer stock to stop home prices rising above 0p1 in figure 2.20 (a).

Data Response 1

Taxicab Licences: the Cartel Case Illustrated

Taxicabs in Civis

In Civis, as elsewhere in the UK, taxicabs are licensed (for a nominal amount) by the local authority. The price per mile charged by the taxis is set by the local authority and is the same for all taxi operators. With the decline in public facilities and the development of a new shopping centre, demand for taxi services has doubled in Civis. This has resulted in the price of taxicab licences rising in the free market, representing a form of monopoly profit (an economic rent of scarcity). In effect it represents the discounted income stream an owner of taxis could earn over time. The authority proposes to increase the number of new licences issued. This move has been met with protest by existing taxicab licence holders.

1. Use figure A (i) and show the extra income generated by the increase in demand. If the number of licences increased, what would happen to this revenue?

Fig. A Demand and Supply for Taxicab Travel and Licenses

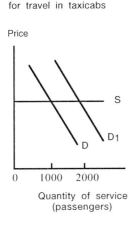

(i) Supply & demand
for travel in taxicabs

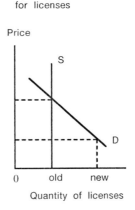

(ii) Supply & demand
for licenses

2. Use figure A(ii) to show the economic profit earned by existing taxicab owners. If the number of licences increases, show the new price for licences and the position of the existing taxicab owners with regard to economic profit earned from owning a licence.

3. Outline the main arguments in favour of limiting/increasing the number of taxi licences.

Data Response 2

Using Market Analysis

Fig XY shows the market for a legal, purchaseable, pain-reducing drug with an equilibrium price of op. Some politicians have suggested the drug should be more widely available and have suggested a lower fixed price of op_1 would be the solution. As an economist you have been asked to advise on the likely impact of this controlled pricing policy.

Fig. XY

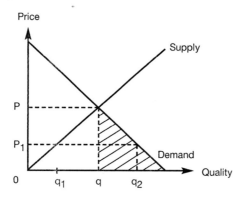

1. Identify the shaded area in Fig XY.

2. Show the impact of the controlled price on (a) the shaded area (b) the free market price.

3. How would you make the drug more widely available? Use the diagram to illustrate.

Data Response 3

The Crisis in the EC's Common Agricultural Policy

Farming in most rich countries is in a classic mess. As food prices have tumbled on world markets, subsidies to farmers (paid through taxes or propped-up food prices) have spiralled to more than $100 billion a year. Such protectionism only sharpens the appetite for more; it never achieves its proclaimed goals. Farmers' incomes and land prices are falling, bankruptcies are rising. Now the Americans have urged the EEC to agree to abolish all subsidies and barriers to agricultural trade within ten years. The Americans have good reasons for wanting a change: their own spending on farm support has trebled in the past three years.

The main way in which the EEC's common agricultural policy supports farmers is by Eurocrats setting guaranteed prices for dairy products, beef, cereals and sugar. If market prices fall below the floor, intervention agencies buy the surpluses. This rigged system is buttressed by import levies and export subsidies, and its benefits go mainly to the wrong people. Three-quarters of EEC farm support reaches the biggest and richest 25% of farmers, concentrated in the wealthier northern countries. They get nearly $10 000 a year each from Europe's taxpayers. The other quarter goes to the poorer, southern 75% of farmers. They get about $1000 a year each. Most distortingly, because German and French politicians want their farmers to have average German and French incomes, the EEC pays Karl and Jacques to produce butter at five times the price at which New Zealanders can do it; some of this butter is dumped on world markets at under one-fifth of its true cost, making economic New Zealand butter unsellable.

Europe's farm ministers recognise some of these absurdities, but prefer to tackle the symptoms (for example through curbing surpluses of milk and sugar by imposing production quotas) rather than the cause (which is the gap between Community prices and world prices). Quotas have sometimes made the gap worse, because farmers have received higher prices to compensate them for not being allowed to produce so much of what is not wanted.* Quotas also freeze market shares. Trading in quotas mitigates this, but creates nonsenses of its own. In parts of Britain a farmer's milk quotas are now worth more than his land. Curbs on milk output can just mean more beef or cereals. When everything is in surplus, quotas are a nightmare of red tape, with each farmer having to account for his production down to the last bunch of radishes.

Every statesman knows that a better solution would be sharp cuts in support prices, but these are called politically impossible.

Source: *The Economist,* 3 October 1987

* A quota system aims to reduce output.

1. Why would the Americans have good reason for wanting a change in the EEC's agricultural policy?

2. Draw a diagram to show the impact of the EEC support policy.

3. How does the trading in quotas reduce the possibility of market shares being frozen? Use the diagram to illustrate.

4. Why does a quota system lead to systematic bureaucracy and accounting?

Data Response 4

Comparative Demand Patterns

(i) Consumers' expenditure on fuel and light

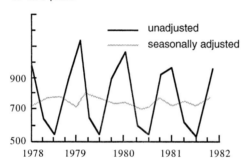

*Source: Economic Progress Report,
The Treasury, March 1983*

(ii) Orders for new houses, 1978-81

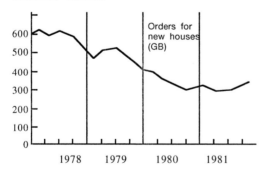

*Source: Economic Trends, CSO,
March 1982*

1. Explain the terms (i) unadjusted (ii) seasonally adjusted (iii) at 1975 prices. What do (ii) and (iii) attempt to do?

2. Outline the main factors affecting the demand for fuel and light and new houses.

3. Compare the behaviour in each diagram and explain the overall difference, using economic analysis.

Data Response 5

Problems in Smallhamlet

A group of market gardeners had for many years sent their tomatoes to be sold at the weekly market in Smallhamlet. However, the Smallhamlet Council decided to ban car parking in the streets near the markets with the result that the number of people shopping in the market decreased substantially. At first the farmers continued to send their tomatoes to the market in the hope that trade might pick up again. However, those farmers living furthest away eventually switched their supplies to Bigtown, where conditions for shopping were more favourable.

Show, by means of a diagram (explaining your diagram with a few sentences), the demand and supply conditions at Smallhamlet:

1. before the parking ban was introduced;

2. immediately after the parking ban was introduced and

3. after some supplies had been switched to Bigtown.

Data Response 6

Using Market Analysis: the Channel Tunnel

Data- The diagram shows the demand (d) and supply (s) conditions for cross channel traffic. The market is in equilibrium with a price of op and the number of trips is given as oq. The demand shifts to d1 and shows how demand for journeys will increase and with no increase in supply the price rises to op1. However a new tunnel means supply increases to S1 and increases capacity.

1. What will be the benefit of the new tunnel for those users who would have made the crossing even if the tunnel did not exist? Shade in the benefit.

2. How many extra journeys will be made because of the tunnel? What is the crucial factor in determining these extra journeys?

3. How would you interpret q2-q?

4. What will be the impact of the Tunnel on (a) cross channel ferry prices; (b) British Rail; (c) Kent?

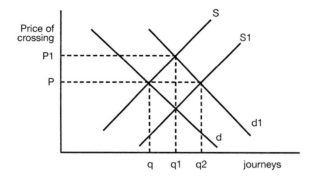

Data Response 7

Study the graphs below and then answer questions (a) to (d).

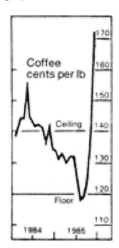

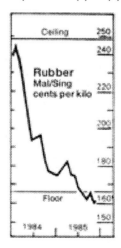

Source: *The Economist*

Trading in the markets for the commodities referred to above is (or has been) affected by the operation of commodity agreements. These agreements attempt to achieve some degree of price stability.

1. Suggest two causes of the price changes for coffee and rubber.

2. What would you understand by the terms' 'ceiling' and 'floor' as used in the above graphs.

3. Using a diagram or diagrams, analyse how the authorities attempt to stabilise the price of one of the commodities shown above.

4. Why is it difficult to make commodity agreements successful?

5. What would be the effect of the price instability in commodity markets on (I) the consuming countries and (ii) the producing countries?

Data Response 8

Price Stabilisation Policies

Figure A shows the market conditions for an agricultural product. Since the actual output fluctuates around the planned output OB, the farmers decide to form a producers' association to stabilise the price at OA and the output at OB.

Fig. A

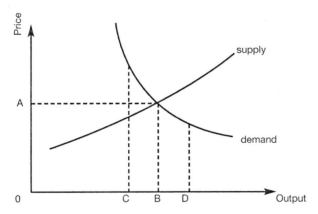

1. Show what the producers' association will do when the actual output is (a) OC and (b) OD.

2. Shade in the average level of producers' income at outputs OC and OD.

3. Under what conditions might the policy adopted by the producers' association fail in the long term?

4. If the government instead of the producers' association attempted to stabilise (i.e.

guarantee price) and output at OA and Ob, what would happen to the producers' income and hence the success of the policy? (Hint: what happens to farmers' income with guarantee price?)

An alternative stabilisation policy is illustrated in figure B. Instead of aiming to stabilise farm prices and output, the government's prime aim is to stabilise income. It buys and sells produce as necessary so that elasticity of demand (E) is unity.

Fig. B

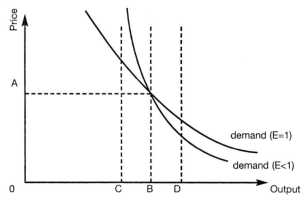

5. Use the diagram to show what the government's action will be when actual farm output is (a) OD; (b) OC and (c) OB.

6. What will happen to price fluctuations with this policy?

7. What practical considerations would have to be borne in mind before either of these policies could be introduced?

Data Response 9
Agricultural Support Policies

The UK deficiency payments scheme (pre-1971)*

Figure C shows the pre-1971 method by which the government subsidised consumers and producers with respect to farm products. The cost of self-sufficiency (SSP) would have been too high so minimum guarantee prices (MGP) were established for farmers. The world price for foodstuffs (WP) was allowed to determine consumption and farmers were encouraged to increase production by means of a subsidy equivalent to (MGP - WP). Thus output was partly home-produced and partly imported.

Fig. C

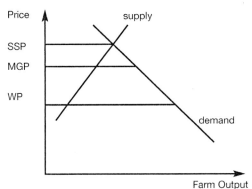

On a copy of figure C show (a) the extra production encouraged by the subsidy: (b) the amount of imports and hence the excess home consumption generated by cheap imports; (c) the 'consumer surplus' generated by cheap imports: (d) the amount of taxation necessary to subsidise consumer food prices; (e) the income provided to third world exporting countries who sold imports to the UK; (f) why the cost of self-sufficiency would have been too high.

Data Response 10

Countries A and B produced and consume good X. Their respective demand and supply schedules are shown. (Assume that no other countries are involved).

Country A			Country B		
Price (£)	Supply	Demand	Price (£)	Supply	Demand
10	100	80	10	140	40
9	90	90	9	130	50
8	80	100	8	120	60
7	70	110	7	110	70
6	60	120	6	100	80
5	50	130	5	90	90

1. What will the price of X be in countries A and B in the absence of trade?

2. If international trade takes place (with no transport costs) what will the world price of X be?

3. At the world price, what will be the value of imports, exports and home production in countries A and B?

4. Country A imposes a tariff of £1 a unit. What will (a) the new world prices (A/B) and (b)

the value of imports and exports?

5. Who will (a) benefit and (b) lose from imposition of the tariff?

Data Response 11

Oil Imports

Countries A and B are both self-sufficient in oil at the currency equivalents of £25 per barrel, and have identical supply and demand conditions (shown by the line S and D on the graphs). They become able to import oil at £15 per barrel, so their consumption of it, adjust accordingly. In attempts to reduce the amount of oil being imported, country A imposes a tariff of £5 per barrel, and country B decides to limit demand by rationing oil (by issuing coupons), thus moving the demand curve from D to D1.

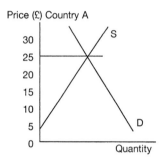

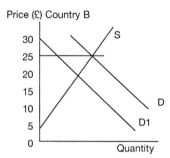

1. Copy the graphs, and show the levels of home production and consumption of oil before the cheaper imported oil became available.

2. Show the effects on home production and demand when oil is imported at £15 per barrel, and the value of imported oil.

3. Compare the impacts of the two import-reducing policies on (a) internal prices; (b) revenues from imported oil; (c) the government's position and (d) home production and consumption.

4. What would happen if some coupon-holders in country B were to sell their ration coupons in the open market?

Data Response 12

Fixed Versus Floating Exchange Rates

The supply and demand curves show how management of the exchange rate affects the amount of US dollar reserves that is needed by a country. In figure A the exchange rate is held fixed at P whereas in figure B it is allowed to float between P and P1.

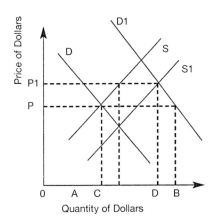

Fig. A   **Fig. B**

1. What might cause the country's demand for dollars to shift from D to D1, in fig. A? What does the distance AB represent?

2. In fig. B the government allows the exchange rate to change to P1 when demand shifts from D to D1. What has happened to the value of its currency? How would the government bring about the necessary shift in the supply of dollars, from S to S1? What does the distance CD represent?

3. If the government allowed fully flexible exchange rates, what would happen to the value of its currency, and to its need for reserves of US dollars?

4. Under what circumstances would managed floating exchange rates be preferred to fixed rates? Can you give examples from the UK's experience to support your argument?

Data Response 13

The Determination of the Value of the Pound

Supply and demand curves for sterling on a particular day

Price of Sterling (in $)	1.50	1.55	1.60	1.64
Sterling Demand (£m)	25	22	20	17
Sterling supplied (£m)	15	17	20	22

1. What will be the equilibrium exchange rate?

2. Britain's trade-figures show a deficit and the demand for pounds falls by £5m. What will the new exchange rate be?

3. In these circumstances, the British authorities decide to peg the exchange rate at £1= 1.60 dollars. What steps do they take to achieve this?

4.   If they were able to peg sterling at this exchange rate, would it be over or under valued?

Data Response 14

Price of pounds ($)

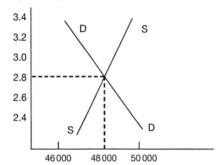

Supply and demand for pounds (£m per annum)

1. What is the equilibrium value of one dollar in terms of the pound?

2. Draw new demand and supply curves, and determine the approximate exchange rate, for the following situations:

a. the government reduces spending on overseas embassies by £500m;

b. the government decides to hold an extra £1000m in sterling balances;

c. overseas navies buy ten new warships from the UK each worth £100m;

d. an end to the UK recession causes firms to spend an extra £500m on imported material stocks.

3. If the government wishes to maintain an exchange rate of £1 = 3 dollars in the original situation, how much official financing would it require and what form might the official financing take?

Multiple Choice

1. There is movement along a demand curve when:

   a. income rises

   b. the population increases

   c. price falls

   d. supply increases and the price of competition goods changes

   e. there are changes in peoples tastes.

2. Each of the following affects the supply of potatoes except:

   a. the cost of fertiliser

   b. the wages of farm labourers

   c. the price of agricultural land

   d. the popularity of crisps

   e. an attack of Colorado Beetle.

3. The movement of the demand curve from DD to D1D1 in figure A might be attributable to:

   a. a switch in demand to a substitute

   b. anticipation of an increase in VAT on the good

   c. a rise in the price of a complementary good

   d. a change in consumer tastes away from the good

   e. a fall in price of the good.

Fig. A

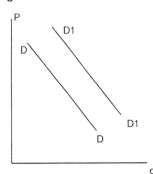

Fig. B

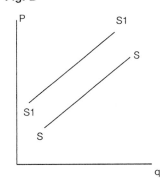

3b. The movement of the supply curve from SS to S1 S1in figure B might be attributable to:

a. a bumper harvest

b. a fall in the costs of production

c. the granting of a subsidy to producers

d. the imposition of a tax on commodity

e. the Government declares a statutory price of OP1.

4. For each of the following questions, choose one option (a,b,c,d or e) which correctly describes the condition illustrated by the graphs (1- 5). Each option may be used once, or not at all.

a. a rise in the quantity supplied caused by a rise in price

b. a rise in price caused by a fall in supply

c. a fall in the price caused by a fall in demand

d. a rise in the quantity demanded caused by the fall in price

e. constant price but changes in demand and supply.

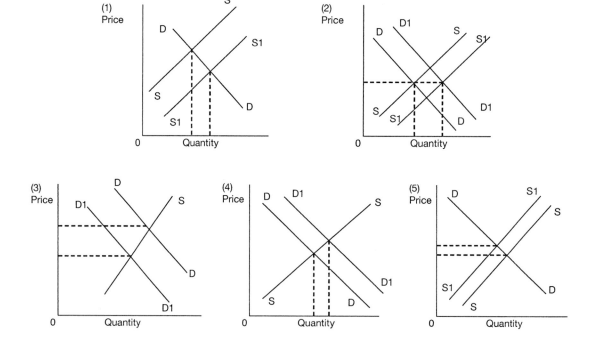

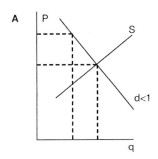

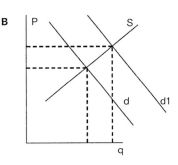

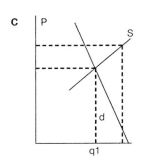

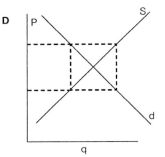

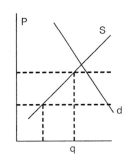

5. The diagram above illustrates the market situation for government policies designed to boost the incomes of producers of certain agricultural commodities.

Match the diagrams A to E to the statements (i) to (v).

(I)   advertising campaigns stressing the nutritional value of certain products

(ii) the imposition of quotas on domestic producers with the intention of restricting quantities produced

(iii) intervention purchasing to ensure that producers receive minimum prices above free market levels eg buffer stock

(iv) a per unit subsidy on a target price set above equilibrium so excess production sold

(v)   a deficiency payment scheme whereby producers receive a subsidy equivalent to the difference between the cheap imported price and a higher guaranteed home price below the equilibrium price.

5 b. Compare the impact of each policy upon producers, consumers and taxpayers by using shaded areas for subsidy, consumer spending and producer income.

6. The diagram below shows the price that successive salmon fisherman would be willing to pay for a ticket to fish a river.

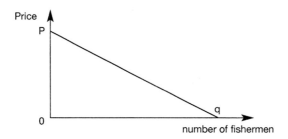

The owner intends to state publicly the number of tickets to be sold (No Price Discrimination) and to sell them at a standard price. What should the owner do to maximise his income?

a. issue as many tickets as there are fishermen

b. restrict the issue of tickets to those prepared to pay price OP

c. issue $\frac{Oq}{2}$ tickets at the highest price they will fetch

d. issue tickets at price OP

e. issue $\frac{Oq}{2}$ tickets at price OP.

7. The diagram below depicts the UK market for coal. The decrease Q1 to Q2 in the equilibrium quantity could be caused by any of the following except:

a. a decrease in the world price of oil

b. an increase in the amount of electricity generated by nuclear power

c. increased production of natural gas from the North Sea

d. a reduction in the number of mines producing coal.

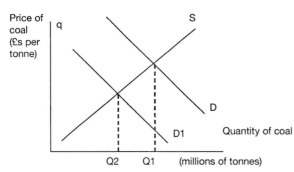

8. The figures in the table below relate to the demand and supply schedules for a good.

price per kg (p)	amount demanded (thousand Kg)	amount supplied (thousand Kg)
30	1	12
25	2	9
20	3	7
15	5	5
10	7	3
5	10	1

The government imposed a fixed price of 25p per Kg and agreed to buy up any unsold produce.

What was its expenditure?

9. Which one of the following might explain a simultaneous increased in both price and quantity traded in the market for a normal price?

a. the removal of a price ceiling on the good

b. a reduction in the tariff levied on imports of the good

c. technological progress in the production of the good

d. the imposition of a tax on the good

e. the granting of a subsidy to producers of the good.

10. The number of passenger journeys per week by train on a certain route is shown by the demand curve QQ in the diagram below.

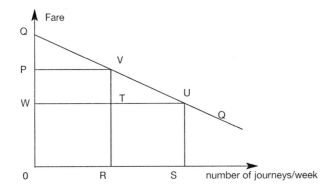

Initially the fare is OP but it is then cut by PW. The loss of revenue from those passengers who would have travelled at the higher fare is shown by the area:

a. PVTW

b. VUT

c. QVUW

d. QPV

e. PVUW

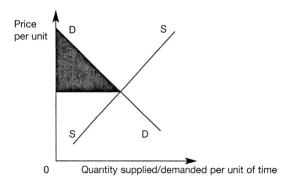

11. The above diagram represents the demand for and supply of golf balls. The shaded area represents the:

   a. normal profit of a monopoly

   b. opportunity costs of golf balls

   c. above normal profits of firms with a local monopoly

   d. profits of a firm with an absolute monopoly

   e. consumers' surplus.

12. Economic theory predicts that controls which set rents for housing which are below the equilibrium price:

   a. will improve the quality of rented property supplied to customers

   b. are an effective method of dealing with excess demand for rented property

   c. will increase the inflation rate

   d. will increase the revenue of property owners

   e. will reduce the quantity supplied of rented property

   f. none of these

Applied Market Economics - Case Studies

Supply and Demand analyses are used in detail to discuss firstly the housing market, and secondly the healthcare market.

The Housing Market 1989 - 1992

The UK housing market is composed of a stock of around 22 million second-hand units, i.e. 98% plus of the total market plus a variable new building programme which can be viewed as a flow depending upon housing starts. Using supply and demand analysis, see figs. A and B, it is possible to deduce the connections between each market.

The second-hand housing stock is shown as S1 in figure A. As demand increases from d0 to d3 due to increasing real incomes, lower interest rates and optimistic expectations, real house prices rise from P1 to P3

Fig. A: Second Hand Housing Market

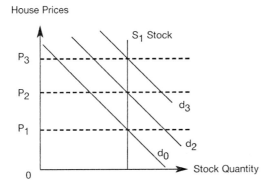

New build supply, S2 in figure B, shadows the second-hand market and is a flow of competitively produced output which initially requires a minimum price of P2 before building commences. This price reflects existing land and construction costs.

Demand conditions as shown with d2 and d3 will be similar in both markets because both markets provide roughly the same product in the eyes of the buyer.

As demand increases, d2 to d3 new build output is stimulated as the stock of housing is increased in value, i.e. P2 to P3 At the same time land values, consumer debt and the Building Societies asset values of the housing stock continue to increase. Mortgage value and turnover from the new housing sector is also buoyant as is the value of potential development land.

Using this analysis the impact of the housing downturn experienced in the UK after 1989 can be unravelled. If the economy achieves demand levels of d3, in both markets, consistent with a price of P3, a sudden reduction in demand to d2 will have a dramatic short run impact.

Fig. B: New Housing Market

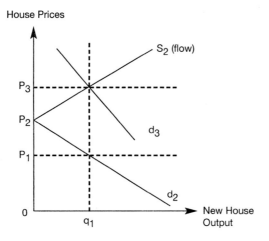

In figure B the finished new build output of Oq1 can only be sold if price now falls to P1, i.e. below the original price of construction and land costs. This could mean financial disaster for builders. Some may hold onto these new houses until times improve or their assets (houses) may go to the receiver and thus again be temporarily removed from the market.

To make matters worse builders who have built up land banks at prices of OP2 will suffer capital losses. The new build market will also influence the second-hand market because the price fall to OP1 will reduce the overall value of the second-hand stock. If would-be sellers in market A try to sell at a price of OP2 then supply at S1 will far exceed the demand of do which has been induced by the temporary new build price of OP1 and the number of 'For Sale' signboards will multiply.

Furthermore the value of Building Society assets will also be affected because these in turn will be roughly the equivalent of the falling value of the mortgaged housing stock. In terms of figure A this fall in value will be from Op3 x OS1 to Op1 x OS1 and for many of the smaller societies it could mean insolvency as the value of their assets (mortgages) falls below house values.

This explains why the larger Building Societies are reluctant to place repossessed homes on to a falling market. In many areas Building Societies would in the above situation effectively operate as a major seller of housing and they would reduce the overall value of their own assets if they rushed to sell these repossessed homes.

In the jargon of the economist, they are monopolists temporarily able to influence the price of the product they trade in. This action is a restrictive practice which may maintain housing values and protect their solvency but does little for first-time buyers wishing to purchase at OP1.

The Market for Health Care (or why the NHS can't win!)

The workings of the NHS are different from the economics of other commodities because of the requirement for healthcare to be provided free. Thus the healthcare market clears by quantity adjustment rather than by price adjustment.

This is explained by considering how healthcare might be provided in a private market i.e., how it was provided prior to the establishment of the NHS. In figure C, the demand for healthcare, D1, is downward sloping, i.e. people demand fewer treatments if the price of treatment rises. If private hospitals decided to supply SA treatments in any one year, then the equilibrium price for medical care would be P1. If demand were to shift against this chosen supply from D1 to D2, then the price would change correspondingly, from P1 to P2. Under the NHS, a market adjustment of this nature does not operate. The NHS supplies healthcare free of charge (i.e. at a zero price). At such a price, B treatments will be demanded according to demand curve D1, and the NHS must therefore supply according to the supply curve SB. The demand rise from D1 to D2 in the NHS case cannot be resolved by a price rise as before, because prices cannot rise. In the face of such a rise, either more resources would have to be put into healthcare to increase supply to SC or (C-B) patients would go untreated, and would join the waiting list for treatment the following year.

Fig. C: Demand and Supply of Health Care

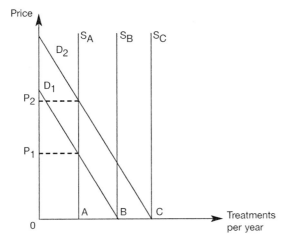

The NHS and the Private Sector

If the public demand for health is D2 and the NHS provides SB then the excess demand C - B could be treated by the NHS using the private sector. In early 2000 the Blair Government announced it would pay the private health sector to do emergency operations in order to cut the NHS waiting lists, i.e. B-C.

Data Question

In diagram 1, S represents the initial stock of rented houses and D represents the demand for rented houses.

In diagram 2, T represents the number of rented houses that are transferred to owner occupation in each period and R the number of new houses built for renting in each period.

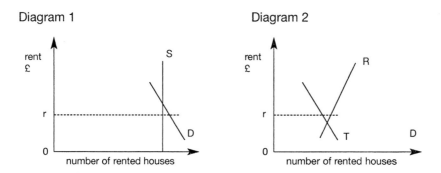

Diagram 1   Diagram 2

If the maximum rent is fixed at 0r, what will be the result?

A   There will be an initial surplus of rented accommodation.

B   There will be a permanent surplus of rented accommodation.

C   There will be a permanent shortage of rented accommodation.

D   The stock of rented housing will decline over time.

E   The stock of rented housing will increase over time.

F   None of the above/

chapter three

Elasticity

Aims

To define, explain and discuss

- Price, Income and Cross Elasticity of Demand
- Factors Influencing Demand Elasticity
- Factors Influencing Supply Elasticity
- Price Variations and Elasticity
- Governments, Taxation and Market Controls

Key Concepts

Price, Income and Cross Elasticity of Demand; Supply Elasticity; Revenue and Elasticity. Buffer Stocks; Incidence of Taxation; Cobweb Theory

Demand elasticity measures the responsiveness of quantity demanded of a good (x) for some given small change in (i) the price of x, (ii) real disposable income, and (iii) the price of a complementary or substitute good (y) or some other variable, for example advertising. Supply elasticity measures the responsiveness of quantity supplied for some small change in the price of the good (x).

Price Elasticity of Demand (PED)

This measures the responsiveness of quantity demanded for some small change in the price or by formula:

The coefficient of elasticity will usually be negative (-) in value since demand falls as price rises and will vary from less than 1 (<1), unity (=1) and then to values greater than one (>1). Inferior goods will be indicated by positive values (+). figure 3.1 shows how demand responds with respect to a small change in price and (i) to (v) indicate the different types of elasticity applying the above formula.

$$\text{PED (at a point)} = \frac{\text{\% change in quantity demanded of x}}{\text{\% change in price of x}} = \begin{array}{l}\text{coefficient of elasticity} \\ \text{- >1 elastic} \\ \text{- <1 inelastic} \\ \text{- =1 unit elasticity}\end{array}$$

If revenue is equal to price (p) x quantity demanded (qD) and price changes as figure 3.1 shows, then revenue will also change. The extent of this revenue change is measured by comparing areas a and b, the shaded area is common. The results of changing revenues with respect to price changes are summarised for 1 to 5:

1. If demand is elastic (D1) and the price rises by 10%, then overall revenue falls. If demand is elastic (D1) and the price falls by 10%, then overall revenue rises.

2. If demand is inelastic (D2) and price rises by 10%, then overall revenue rises. If demand is inelastic (D2) and prices fall by 10%, then overall revenue falls.

3. If demand is unity (D3) and the price rises or falls by 10%, then overall revenue remains constant.

4. If demand is completely inelastic (D4) and price rises by 10%, then overall revenue rises. If demand is completely inelastic (D4) and price falls by 10%, then overall revenue falls.

5. If demand is completely elastic (D5) and price rises or falls by 10%, then revenue increases or reduces by an infinite amount.

Fig. 3.1   Graphical Illustration of Demand Elasticity (with respect to small price changes)

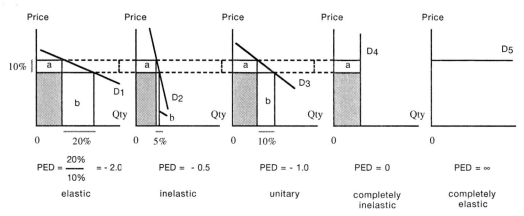

Demand Elasticity and the Gradient of a Curve

The simple graphical concept of elasticity stresses how demand responsiveness varies but each price change has to be seen as a very small change over the total demand schedule. This is because, on a demand schedule, elasticity will be different between different prices so it is not the same as the gradient of the line. With reference to figure 3.2, consider a change from 8p to 10p which reduces demand from 20 to 10 units. These are changes of 25% and 100% respectively, that is elasticity equals - 4 (elastic). However, the price change from 2p to 3p leads to a quantity change of 50 to 60, percentage changes of 50% and 20%, that is elasticity equals - 0.4 (inelastic). Thus the line in figure 3.2 appears to have the same gradient but elasticity varies along it. In the same way, whilst PED from 2p to 3p is - 0.44, from 3p to 2p PED is equal to a price change of 33.333%, a quantity change of 20% so elasticity equals $^{20\%}/_{33.333\%}$ = - 0.6.

Thus elasticity depends upon whether the change is from 2p to 3p or 3p to 2p. The correct procedure is to take both values and divide by 2, 0.4 + 0.6 = 1/2 = - 0.5. However, for practical purposes, elasticity is normally worked on the original price change, that is from 2p to 3p.

Fig. 3.2 Demand Elasticity

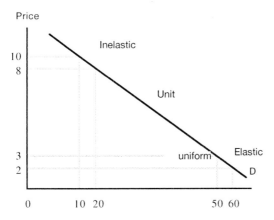

Determinants of Demand Elasticity: with Respect to Price

Degree of Substitutability

The easier it is to substitute the good for another, the more elastic demand will be with respect to price. Thus whilst demand for food may be inelastic overall the demand for butter or margarine may be very elastic as they can be substituted for each other and for other brands of margarine or butter.

The Time Factor

In the short term it is often difficult to quickly obtain a substitute good, but in the long term consumers will adapt their behaviour, and alternatives will be available so demand becomes more elastic as consumers are able to buy more alternatives.

Luxury Versus Necessity

It is sometimes argued that the more a good is a basic necessity the more inelastic demand becomes, whilst for a luxury demand will be more elastic. However, in affluent economies a luxury, such as a motor car, is perceived by many as a necessity.

The Amount of Consumers' Income Spent on the Good

If only a small amount of consumers' income is spent on a good then demand will be inelastic. A once-yearly purchase of shoe laces which increase in price from 20p to 30p is hardly likely to reduce demand. A rise in the cost of house mortgage, which takes up a large amount of the household budget, will reduce demand for housing.

The Structure of the Market

Whilst a competitive supplier will face a completely elastic demand, a monopolist faces a more elastic demand for his product. In fact, intensive advertising can mean the demand for the monopolist's product becomes more and more inelastic.

Elasticity of Supply (ES)

This measures the responsiveness of quantity supplied to a change in price. It is the relationship between the proportionate change in price and the proportionate change in quantity supplied. The formula is:

$$ES \text{ (at a point)} = \frac{\text{\% change in quantity supplied of x}}{\text{\% change in price of x}} = \begin{array}{l} \text{coefficient of elasticity} \\ +>1 \text{ elastic} \\ +<1 \text{ inelastic} \\ +=1 \text{ unit elasticity} \end{array}$$

Since supply increases with price, the relationship is positive (+) and varies from inelastic to elastic with other types of elasticity illustrated in figure 3.3 (i) to (v). Elasticity of supply is very important in explaining economic rent and transfer earnings.

Fig. 3.3 Graphical Illustration of Supply Elasticity

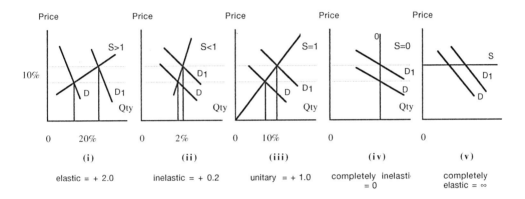

(i)	(ii)	(iii)	(iv)	(v)
elastic = + 2.0	inelastic = + 0.2	unitary = + 1.0	completely inelastic = 0	completely elastic = ∞

Factors Influencing Elasticity of Supply

Time

In the very short term the industry (firm) cannot increase the fixed or variable factor very easily so supply will be inelastic. In the shortrun the variable factor can be increased and in the long run all factor proportions can change. The above refers to the flow of goods and services. The stock of land or valuable paintings is often fixed in all but the very longterm.

Factor or Product Capacity

If there are unemployed variable factors, such as labour, then firms will be able to expand production easily so supply is elastic. If it is possible to import labour or even products, then supply becomes more elastic; imports are perfectly elastic at the world price.

Production and Training Delays

In the case of certain agricultural and labour markets, there is often a considerable time lag between the planting of a crop and its harvesting, and its supply is inelastic in the short term but elastic in the long run. The supply of trained personnel is fixed at one time because it takes time to train new recruits. Once trained, supply now becomes more elastic.

Capital Investment

In heavy capital investment industries, such as chemicals, it takes time for the investment to come on-stream and become fully operational. Once on-line it then takes time and a heavy capital investment before expansion can be increased. This is also true with respect to the opening up of new mines or oilwells. The impact of a rise in demand for these products is a sharp increase in price in the short-term because supply is inelastic. In many product markets 'bottlenecks' appear which push up price and only if stocks can be drawn upon will these problems disappear. Once stocks have been used up, supply then becomes very limited (inelastic).

Income Elasticity of Demand (YED)

This measures the response of demand for a good to a change in real disposable income by formula:

$$\text{YED (at a point)} = \frac{\text{\% change in quantity demanded of } x}{\text{\% change in real income}} = \begin{array}{l} \text{coefficient of} \\ \text{elasticity} \\ \text{+1 unity} \\ \text{<1 inelastic} \\ \text{>1 elastic} \\ \text{- inferior} \end{array}$$

These are illustrated in figure 3.4 (i) where schedules A, B and C illustrate normal goods and where D illustrates an inferior good. In the West, goods such as TVs, videos, cars and capital goods are likely to be elastic with respect to income so in times of booms and slumps demand for the goods is likely to behave in an erratic fashion. However, for heating and food stuffs generally, demand is more stable and inelastic. Inferior goods, such as cigarettes, are those where, for example, high income groups spend less proportionately than lower income groups. Figure 3.4 (ii) shows how, for some given price, real income increases lead to changes or shifts in demand depending upon the type of income elasticity, that is A to D. Original demand is at O.

Fig. 3.4 Income Elasticity

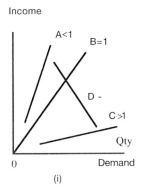

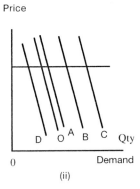

(i)   (ii)

Cross Elasticity of Demand (CED)

This measures the responsiveness of the demand for one good with respect to the price of another, which may be a substitute or a complement. For substitutes the formula gives a (+) or direct relationship and for complements a (-) or negative relationship. The degree of substitutability or complementary is indicated by the value of the coefficient. The larger the value, the closer the relationship. The formula for CED is the same for both complements and substitutes and is:

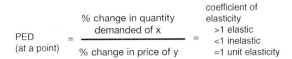

Figure 3.5 (i) shows petrol and cars as complements and how elasticity behaves whilst (ii) illustrates tea and coffee as substitutes. Price and income elasticities are given in Tables 3.1 and 3.2 for the UK for 1981-86 and 1960-85 in order to illustrate how food elasticities vary.

Fig. 3.5 Cross Elasticity

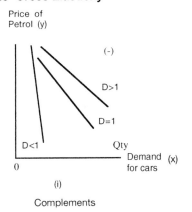

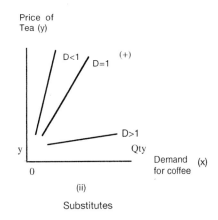

(i)   (ii)

Complements   Substitutes

Table 3.1 Estimated Price Elasticities of Demand for Selected Foods in the UK 1981-86

Beef and Veal	- 1.46
Mutton and Lamb	- 1.67
Pork	- 2.01
Frozen Peas	- 0.88
Bread	- 0.26
Tea	- 0.19
Potatoes	- 1.46

Source: Annual Report of the National Food Survey
Committee, Ministry of Agriculture, Fisheries and Foc
Household Food Consumption and Expenditure 1986
(HMSO, 1987)

Table 3.2 Income Elasticities of Demand for Selected Foods in the UK 1960-85

	1960	1975	1985
Beef and Veal	0.16	0.25	0.26
Mutton and Lamb	0.38	0.21	0.19
Pork	0.46	0.39	0.14
Frozen Peas	1.53	0.43	0.33
Bread	- 0.09	0.01	- 0.06
Tea	0.03	- 0.10	- 0.32
Potatoes	0.07	0.01	- 0.23

Source: Annual Report of the National Food Survey
Committee, Ministry of Agriculture, Fisheries and Food,
Household Food Consumption and Expenditure 1986
(HMSO, various years)

Applications of Elasticity

The Incidence of a Tax or Cost of Production Increase

The 'incidence' of a tax on a good, or an increase in the cost of production, refers to who actually pays. Figure 3.6 illustrates a tax/cost increase which shifts supply to S1 and so price rises to 0p1. At the new price the tax to be paid is a - b. Since price has risen from 0p to 0p1, the consumer pays x amount but this still leaves the producer having to pay the difference, y. A rise in costs can also be analysed in this way. A fall in tax, a subsidy or a cost reduction will benefit both consumer and producer by the same amounts, x and y. The incidence of tax or cost increase depends upon the relative elasticity of demand and supply as shown in figure 3.7 (i) to (iv).

Fig. 3.6 The Incidence of Tax

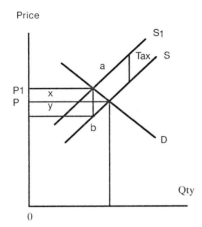

Fig. 3.7 Relative Elasticity & the Incidence of Taxation

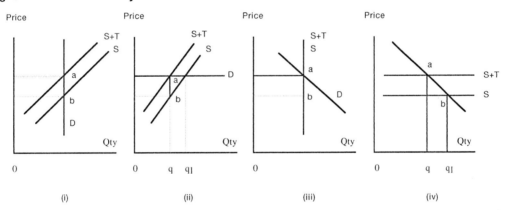

(i)   (ii)   (iii)   (iv)

(i) When demand is completely inelastic the tax is equivalent to the extra price consumers pay, so the consumers pay all the tax and output is unaffected; the tax is neutral.

(ii) When demand is completely elastic, the price stays at p but the tax of a - b has to be paid by the producer. Output and employment will also fall (0q1 - 0q).

(iii) When supply is completely inelastic supply does not change and the price remains at p. The tax a - b is paid by the producer.

(iv) When supply is completely elastic, then S goes to S + T and the consumer pays the tax a - b which is the same as the price rise 0p - 0p1. Output falls, 0q1 - 0q.

The same analysis can be used for a subsidy, which shifts S + T to S in terms of who benefits. At the same time a rise in the cost of production can be analysed as having the same impact as a tax increase.

Specific or Ad Valorum Tax

A specific tax is a lump sum tax which increases the selling price by the same amount regardless of output (value), that is S to S1(see figure 3.8). However, an ad valorum tax will rise as the price increases. This is because 10% of £1, 10p, is less than 10% of £10, i.e. £1. This is reflected in a disproportionate rise in the tax as price increases, S1 to S2.

Fig. 3.8 Taxation

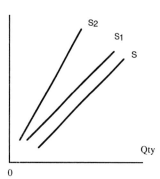

Agricultural Fluctuations Due to Inelastic Demand and Supply

Demand for many agricultural products is inelastic, see figure 3.9 (i), and unforeseen supply changes due to for example a poor harvest; will cause price to fluctuate between 0p and 0p1. This will also increase revenue into the industry but will have little effect upon output, that is 0q1 to 0q. In the event of a good harvest the price fall will substantially reduce producers' income, so governments try to stabilise both price and producers' incomes by buffer stock schemes. In figure 3.9 (ii) it is the inelasticity of supply together with fluctuations in demand which changes price, output and hence industry revenue. Again some buffer stock scheme or agricultural support policy could be used to stabilise price and income.

Fig. 3.9 Agricultural Price Fluctuations

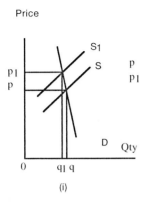

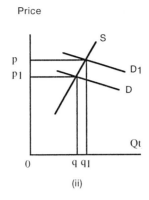

(i)   (ii)

Erratic Price Fluctuations - The Cobweb Theory

Originally confined to agricultural markets, the cobweb theory combines market price instability and the concept of elasticity in order to explain price behaviour patterns which are illustrated in figure 3.10 A, B, (i) to (iii) with respect to price and demand analysis. The behaviour of market prices is shown in row A and displays a variety of forms. In row B the corresponding market cobweb is shown. The original cobweb theory made use of a simple idea that there was a time lag between producers recognising and reacting to market price, and the eventual output coming onto the market. Thus if supply depends upon yesterday's price but demand reacts to today's price, it is quite possible for actual demand and planned supply never to coincide. In B (i) assume a planned equilibrium of 0p/0q but then actual output drops to 0q1 due to a bad harvest or because of earlier uncertainty on the part of the farmer. This output of 0q will be forced up in price to 0p and producers will eventually supply 0q2 which then will fall in price to 0p in order to clear this output level supplied. In each case suppliers mistakenly believe p and p2 are the correct market, and hence equilibrium, price, but they are unable to adjust quickly enough (because of the time lag in growing the output) and hence they are unable to correct the problem quickly enough. When demand and supply elasticities are the same, that is 1, the price moves in a regular way. When, as in A and B (ii) supply elasticity is greater than 1 and demand elasticity less than 1, then price instability worsens and price explodes. However, price gradually converges in A and B (iii) when supply elasticity is less than 1 and demand elasticity greater than 1. Any market can behave in this way if suppliers are unable to adapt to market price conditions or if they believe incorrectly that current market price is always equilibrium price. Only correct market information can help them settle on a stable level at 0q and this can come about by improved market research or a more intelligent adaptation to market information, assuming this is up to date and reliable.

Fig. 3.10 Erratic Price Fluctuations: The Cobweb Theory

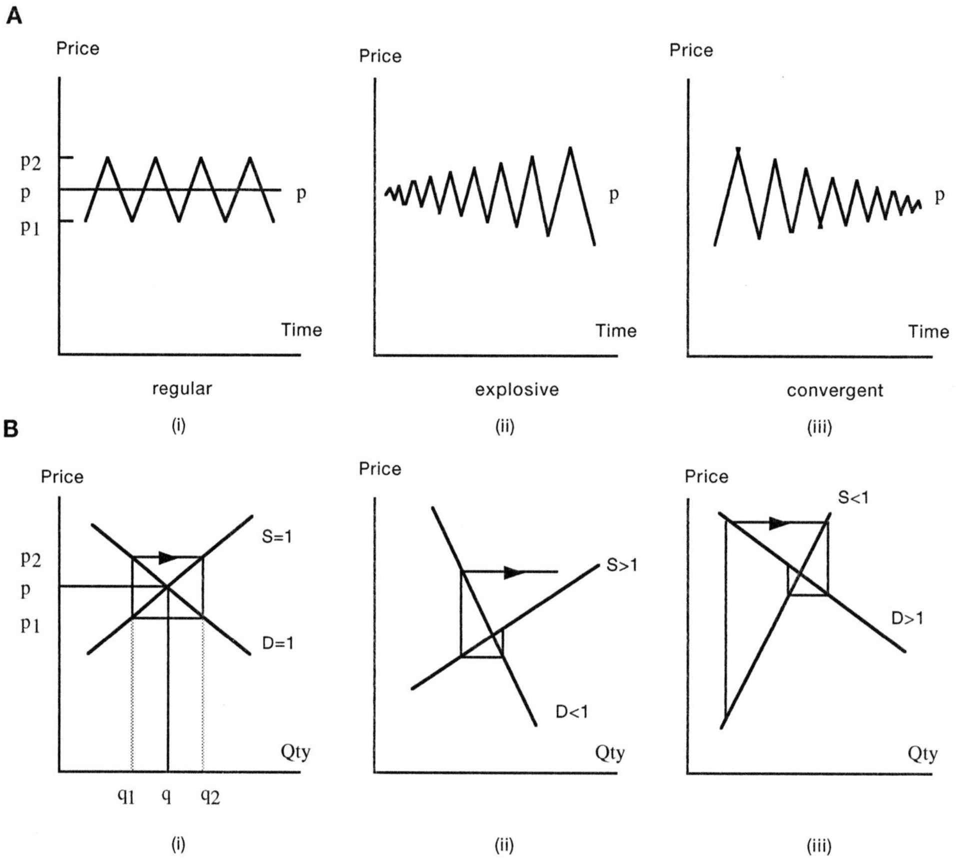

A

regular
(i)

explosive
(ii)

convergent
(iii)

B

(i)

(ii)

(iii)

Research Tasks

1. Survey members of your class, family or friends and collect information regarding how much petrol, bread, sweets or foreign travel would be purchased if the price of each rose/fell. Present your findings in tabular and graphical form.

2. Obtain heating, electricity or goods bills for the year/s and calculate how demand has changed for each product over the year and between years, if records are available. Compare to changes in income and price. Comment.

Data Response 1

Price Elasticity and the Brand Lifecycle

1. Compare the relative price elasticities of detergents and pharmaceuticals over their respective lifecycles.

2. How could businessmen use this information?

3. Explain the meaning of the 'brand lifecycle stage'.

Average Coefficients of Price Elasticity for Several Brands of Detergents and Pharmaceuticals

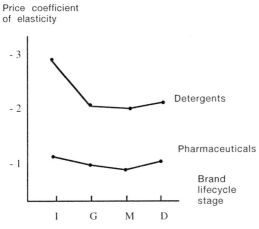

Key: I=Introduction; G=Growth; M=Maturity; D=Decline

Data Response 2

Price Elasticity of Demand in Ruritania

In Ruritania, a hypothetical country whose currency is the pound sterling (£), the three firms in the car industry together sold in 1985 12 million cars at an average price of £5,000. However, because the economy is in a depressed state the car industry is not working at full capacity and many car workers are not employed for a full working week.

The car workers' union, Vehicle and General Workers, suggest that each producer reduces his price by £200. This action, the union argues, would result in another 2 million cars being sold while aggregate profits would be maintained at £4,000 million

1. Calculate the value of the elasticity of demand (correct to one decimal place) assumed by the Vehicle and General Workers Union. Comment on this value.

2. Calculate the average cost with an output of (i) 12 million cars and (ii) 14 million cars. Comment on your findings.

3. A spokesperson for the Ruritanian car industry points out that government economists have estimated that the elasticity of demand for cars is, in

fact, - 0.5. Assuming this estimate is accurate, and given the cost conditions assumed in above, what would be the impact on the car industry's profitability of a price reduction of £200? 4. Other than in the manner suggested by the union, how might Ruritania's car firmstry to increase their sales of cars by acting (i) individually and (ii) as a group?

(London, June 1986)

Data Response 3

Demand Factors: The Lydia Pinkham Case

The Economic Background

Lydia Pinkham's Vegetable Compound is a legendary proprietary medicine which has been intensively advertised in both the press and the media in the USA for many years. It is one of the few marketed products for which sales, advertising and price information have been widely and reliably recorded, while the packaging, ingredients and appeal have changed very little. Thus it provides a unique insight into demand influences over time.

1. Identify the main influence on sales over the period 1908-60.

2. Comment on the apparent overall advertising elasticity of demand for the product between l915-25 and 1945-55.

3. What market explanations can you offer for the relative decline in sales since 1945?

Sales of Lydia Pinkham Company and Disposable Income, 1908-60

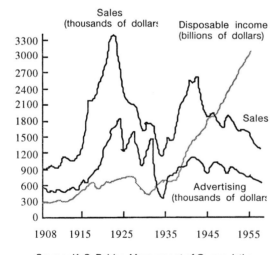

Source: K. S. Palder, *Measurment of Cummulative Advertising Effects*, Prentice Hall

Data Response 4

Cartelisation of Copper

There has much much speculation whether oil represents a special case or whether OPEC might be copied by other commodity groups. In particular, likely candidates for cartelisation have been suggested in metallic industries, and one commodity frequently referred to is copper.

The price of copper is usually very sensitive to fluctuations in the business cycle because of its importance to industries such as electronics, construction and transport. The USA is largely self-sufficient in copper and is one of the world's largest producers. It is not a major exporter of copper and the same is true of socialist countries. About 70% of copper exports are controlled by a group of producers who, in 1967, formed Conseil Intergouvernmental des Pays Exportateurs de Cuivre (CIPEC). This includes Chile, Peru, Zambia and Zaire. CIPEC aims to coordinate the behaviour of members in order to ensure 'continuous increase in growth of real earnings from copper exports'. Despite some favourable characteristics, CIPEC faces some formidable difficulties. Price stability would require cooperation among a variety of countries. Copper exports represent about 90% of Zambia's total export earnings, for Chile 70%, for Zaire 65% and for Peru 20%. Copper demand is expected to rise by about 4% per annum, and short run price elasticity of demand has been estimated at - 1.0.

If CIPEC is compared to OPEC, it is evident that oil exporting countries have a particular advantage in that their product cannot be recycled.

1. Why is the price of copper 'usually very sensitive to fluctuations in the business cycle' (lines 5-6)?

2. What would be the effect on producers' revenue if CIPEC raised copper prices:

    a. In the short run, when price elasticity of demand for copper was - 1.0;

    b. In the long run, if price elasticity of demand for copper was - 2.0 at all prices?

3. Why would you expect the long-run elasticity of demand for copper to exceed its short-run elasticity ?

4. With reference to the passage, examine some of the problems that face CIPEC when the member countries differ over their reliance on copper export earnings.

5. What might a group such as CIPEC achieve, other than the enhancement of revenue through supply restrictions?

Data Response 5

The data below gives estimates of the elasticity of demand for selected foods in the UK.

Income elasticity of demand

All foods	0.10
Beef	0.26
Margarine	-0.22
Fresh Potatoes	-0.43
Fruit Juices	0.95
Bread	-0.18

Price elasticity of demand

Beef	-1.24
Bread	-0.25
Fresh Potatoes	-0.14
Fruit Juices	-0.65
Margarine	-0.37

Cross elasticities of demand for beef and pork

beef with respect to the price of pork	0.10
pork with respect to the price of beef	0.25

Source: 'Household Food Consumption Expenditure', Annual Report of the Food Survey Committee, 1987,HMSSO. C.S.O.

1. With reference to the data, explain why,

   a. all the price elasticities of demand are negative

   b. some income elasticities of demand are positive and some are negative

   c. beef has a high price elasticity of demand but a relatively low income elasticity of demand.

2. a. Explain what is meant by the term 'cross elasticity of demand'.

   b. Comment on the values shown in the table for the cross elasticity of demand for beef and pork.

3. It is expected that levels of income in the UK will rise It is likely that large food retailers will wish to take account of the data on elasticities in their marketing decisions.

    a. Explain, with examples, what uses might be made of the data by large food retailers.

    b. Comment on the likely limitations of the data for their purposes.

Data Response 6

UK Income Elasticity of Demand 1971-81

The table below refers to the income and expenditure of United Kingdom households that contain one man, one woman and two children in 1971 and 1981. Study the table carefully and then, making use of both the data and your knowledge or economics, answer the following questions.

1. Using the data for 1981:

    a. assess whether income and tax and national insurance contributions were progressive in 1981;

    b. using the concept of income elasticity of demand, describe how the expenditure on each of the commodity groups varies with income.

2. Using the data for the average income group:

    a. how has the relation between total and disposable income changed between 1971 and 1981?

    b. describe the changes in the changes in expenditure between 1971 and 1981;

    c. what factors could account for the changes in (ii)?

	1981 Household Income and Expenditure £ per week					Average Income group			
						£ per week		£ per week % of Disposable Income	
						1971	1981	1971	1981
Income Total Income	111.9	164.0	194.8	240.1	327.3	38.3	194.8	114.1	120.9
Income Tax	6.6	16.4	25.2	34.4	58.6	3.3	25.2	9.8	15.6
National Insurance Contributions	3.4	6.4	8.5	10.5	11.3	1.6	8.5	4.6	5.3
Disposable Income	109.9	141.2	161.1	195.2	257.4	33.4	161.4	100.0	100.0
Expenditure on:									
Fuel, light and power	8.0	7.5	8.3	8.6	10.7	1.9	8.3	5.6	5.2
Food	28.3	31.5	33.6	37.0	41.5	8.9	33.6	26.6	20.9
Alcoholic drink	4.4	5.0	5.8	6.1	8.1	1.1	5.8	3.2	3.6
Tobacco	5.2	4.6	3.7	3.4	3.4	1.3	3.7	3.9	2.3
Transport and vehicles	12.2	16.0	18.2	27.1	32.3	1.9	14.6	5.8	9.1
Services	6.7	11.2	14.6	18.7	26.8	1.9	14.6	5.8	9.1

Source: C.S.O.

Multiple Choice

1. **Demand/Supply Schedule in a Market**

Price (P)	Demand	Supply
12	120	300
11	140	260
10	160	220
9	180	180
8	200	140

Use the above schedule to answer:

(i) If a tax of 3p is imposed, the new equilibrium price is:

a) 12p; b) 11p; c) 10p; d) 9p; e) 8p.

(ii) Demand is inelastic within the price range:

a) 11-12p; b) 10-11p; c) 9-10p; d) 8-9p; e) 8-12p.

(iii) If demand increased by 60 at all prices the new equilibrium will be:

a) 8p; b) 10p; c) 11p; d)12p.

2. Two goods, X and Y, are complementary goods. Column T1 of the table below shows the market situation at time period 1 and column T2 shows the situation following and increase in the price of good Y.

	T1	T2
Price of good X	10	10
quantity demanded	50	40
Price of good Y	20	30
quantity demanded	80	60

The value of the cross elasticity of demand for good X lies between:

a. -1.7 and -2.6

b. -0.8 and -1.3

c. -0.3 and -0.8

d. +0.3 and +0.6

e. +1.7 and +2.6

f. -1.7 and +2.6

3. Products X and Y are both produced in Perfectly Competitive product markets using unskilled labour obtained from a Perfectly Competitive labour market.

X has an income elasticity of demand = -0.5

Y has an income elasticity of demand = 0.5

Firms produce either product X or Y, and initially all firms within each industry are at a long run equilibrium.

Over the next year there occurs an increase of 20% in the average consumer disposable income.

a. What term would be used to describe good X?

b. Calculate how the change in income will affect the demand for each good.

c. Describe, with the help of relevant diagrams, the changes which will occur over time in the above product and factor markets.

d. Why might a problem occur if labour were occupationally immobile?

4. The following demand schedule shows the number of flats in an area which would be rented at various monthly rent levels.

Rent	Number of Flats
(£)	demand
140	80
160	70
180	50
200	40
220	30
240	20

If the going rent is £160, what is the elasticity of demand for:

a. a fall of £20 in the monthly rent?

b. a rise in the rent of £40?

5. The suppliers of a certain building material are willing to put the following quantities on the market at the particular prices.

Price (£)	10	9	8	7	6
Quantity supplied (units)	280	225	170	130	110

Calculate the elasticity of supply:

    a. for a price fall from £10 to £9.

    b. for a price rise from £6 to £8.

6. The demand curve for good X is known to be of unitary elasticity. At a price of £6, quantity demanded is 2,000 units. At what price will the quantity be 10,000 units?

    a. £30

    b. £10

    c. £1.33

    d. £1.20

    e. £1.00

    f. £1.10

7. The following table gives an individuals demand for five goods. A, B, C, D and E, at two income levels.

income level	units of goods demanded				
	A	B	C	D	E
£1,000	50	50	50	50	50
£1,100	60	55	52	50	48

Over this range of income for which good does the individual have an income elasticity of demand of unity?

8. One of the assumptions underlying the kinked demand curve is that oligopolists:

    a. sell to consumers who are less sensitive to price increases than price decreases

    b. expect their rivals to match any reduction in price

    c. leave their prices unchanged if a competitor reduces his price.

9. If the income elasticity of demand for a product is +0.3 then:

    a. a rise in real incomes will lead to a fall in demand

    b. a fall in real incomes will lead to a proportionately larger fall in demand

    c. a rise in real incomes will lead to a proportionately larger rise in demand

    d. a fall in real incomes will lead to a proportionately smaller fall in demand

    e. a fall in real incomes will cause a rise in price.

10. The owners of a television cable franchise estimate that the price elasticity of demand for subscriptions to a package of channels is equal to -2.0. They anticipate 5,000 subscribers in a city if price is set at £10 per week. Reducing price to £9 can be expected to change revenue by:

    a. -£5,000 per week

    b. -£4,000 per week

    c. -£1,000 per week

    d. +£4,000 per week

    e. +£5,000 per week

    f. none of these.

11. Under which of the following circumstances would an increase in the price if product X result in a fall in the demand for product Y?

    a. The demand for Y is income inelastic

    b. Y is an inferior good

    c. X and Y are complimentary goods

    d. X and Y are substitutes

    e. the demand for Y is inelastic.

12. Intensive brand product advertising is likely to:-

    a. Shift demand to the right

    b. Make price elasticity of demand increase

    c. Generally make the competitors demand more price elastic

    d. Lead to brand loyalty and product differentiation.

chapter four

Factor Markets

Aims

To define, explain and discuss

- Markets and Functions
- Price Determination
- Application and Evaluation of Market Analysis

Key Concepts

Demand; Supply; Equilibrium Price; Substitutes; Complements; Income; Expectations;Price Controls; Perverse Demand; Buffer Stocks; Market Failure; Product Factor Goods; Market Links

In competitive factor markets the respective prices of labour, land and capital, determined by supply and demand forces, will be wages, rent and interest. The rewards these factors receive will be treated, using market analysis, in the same way as if the market was for a product, for example widgets. Competitive markets for labour, land and capital are characterised by the following:

- Buyers and sellers of factor inputs are price takers; there are no monopoly buyers or sellers.
- Labour and other factors are homogeneous or identical.
- There is full information about the price and quality of factor inputs.
- Factor prices are freely allowed to fluctuate in order to equate demand and supply.
- There is free mobility of factors, for example labour can and will move freely between regions, occupations and industries.

- Factor inputs move in order to receive their highest income and best employment.
- Entrepreneurs employ factors in order to maximise the profits of the business.

Wage Determination: the Competitive Labour Market

In figure 4.1 the short-term wage level and employment levels are given by D/S: £70 and 70 workers.

Fig. 4.1 Wage Determination

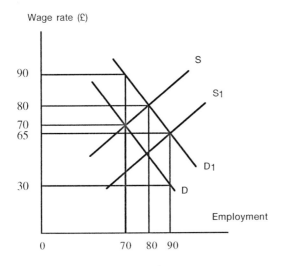

Note. If sex discrimination occurs then S is supply of men and women but demand differs. Demand for men and women are D1 D respectively. Women receive £70, men £80 and abolition mean both earn £80.

Short-term supply of labour reflects:

- Alternative employment opportunities.
- Labour mobility ie geographical and occupational.
  - i. In the very short term, labour supply will be immobile and hence relatively inelastic. Thus D to D1 and wages increase to £90.
  - ii. In the long term, labour supply can increase to S1/D1 (hence the wage/employment levels change to £65 and 90 workers) if, (a) the overall workforce increases, (b) unemployment within the economy increases, (c) women, the elderly or others are trained to work and demand increases.

The derived demand for labour (D), in the short term reflects:

- Demand for the final product. If this is inelastic, labour demand will also be inelastic.
- The price and profitability of the employing industry.
- Falling labour productivity down the demand schedule; as more are employed the wage rate (the value of the worker) falls.

In the long term, the demand and supply can shift to D1, S1 and long-term wage and employment rates will be £65 and 90 workers. This will be because:

- Overall labour/industry productivity increases.
- Demand and price of final product increases.
- Supply shifts from S to S1 due to the factors outlined above.

Impact of Trade Unions, Sole Employers:

Trade unions can influence labour markets and keep wages temporarily above free market rates by limiting entry and hence forcing up wages. At the same time, a dominant or sole employer can force wages below market equilibrium for a level of employment and also discriminate between workers, so paying each worker less than the free market rate. Trade unions can correct these practices if a single wage rate can be negotiated. This is analysed as follows. The competitive labour market, shown in figure 4.1, with wage/employment rates of £70/70 people, could be distorted by an imposed union rate of £80, which then leads to fewer people being employed, i.e. unemployment. Alternatively, a sole employer could employ 90 people, see D1, and pay less than £65 ie £30 as there are no alternative employment opportunities available. Unions can negotiate a wage above £30 ie up to £65.

Demand and Factor Elasticity

Consider two industries A and B in figure 4.1(a) employing the same factor, labour, but their respective demand schedules da/db have different demand elasticities. This means that for any given fall in the wage rate more of the factor is employed by industry B than by industry A, i.e. if the price of labour falls from £10 to £8 industry B's demand for labour increases from 40 to 100 whilst industry A's increase from 40 to 50. The reverse would happen if the wage rose from £8 to £10. Factor elasticity of demand is important and will depend upon:

- The elasticity of demand for the final product. The more elastic the demand for the final product then the more elastic the demand for labour becomes.
- The substitutability of one factor for another. The more substitutable the cheaper factor is in terms of other factors, then the more elastic its demand becomes.

- The amount of factor cost proportion represents in terms of the final cost bill. In industry A the labour factor cost is less important than in industry B in terms of their overall costs.

- The profitability of the industry. If an industry is making large profits it will have an inelastic demand for the factor because even if factor price increases it will be able to afford these extra costs. Less profitable industries will have a more elastic demand schedule.

- The time factor. In the shortterm it is more difficult to substitute other factors for labour when the wage rate increases. However, in the longterm a firm will be able to respond by using others factors if the wage rate rises. This means demand will be inelastic in the shortterm and elastic in the longterm.

- The political climate. If wage increases can be passed on to the customer, then inflationary price increases are expected by customers, so large wage increases can be more easily negotiated by unions when it is believed that governments relax controls on inflation, e.g. at an election time.

Figure 4.1(a)   Factor Demand Elasticities

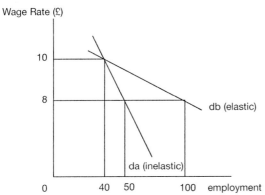

Rent or Land Value Determination

Land is fixed in its physical supply (S) and if it has only one use then its supply will be inelastic (see fig. 4.2). Hence its value is determined by demand which is derived from the profit which can be extracted from its use. Demand for land is influenced by:

- The price, productivity and profit derived from the output of the land.

- The number of competing uses bidding for land.

- Planning controls which limit the uses which the land can be put to.

In figure 4.2, the demand for land can increase from D to D1, (so pushing up the rent from £80 to £100) if (i) the price of the product produced rises or (ii) another use outbids the existing demand or (iii) demand for the same type of land varies between regions.

Fig. 4.2 Rent Determination

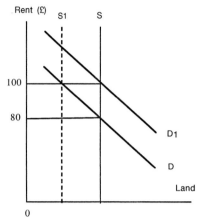

Note:-

(1) Planning controls can allow demand line to change D to D1.

(2) Planning controls can restrict supply to S1 and so push up rents.

When land is not fixed in use, for example it can be used for both residential or agricultural use, then it will move to the highest bidder. The supply curve in each sector will be upward sloping, both because of the different locations and because of the costs involved in transferring from one use to another. If the demand for housing increases from D to D1 (see figure 4.3) and pushes up the price to £80, then land will move from agricultural use (S to S1) and this amount, 10 acres, will enable demand to be met in the housing market. Supply is no longer inelastic.

Fig. 4.3 Alternative Uses for Land

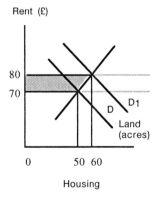 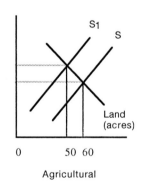

Housing   Agricultural

Economic Rent

In the example, the existing land in housing, previously paid £70, now receives an extra £10 due to demand increasing. Of the £80 now received by the original 50 acres, £70 had to be paid to stop it changing use - its *transfer earnings*. The extra £10 paid, represents £10 economic rent - the shaded area. This analysis can be applied to labour markets and, in terms of inelastic land, all the payment is an economic rent since it has no alternative use.

Economic Rent - Quasi Profit

When the supply of capital is fixed in the short term and supply is inelastic then demand pressures will push up interest and hence profit rates of return. This increase in profit is known as quasi-profit and is a form of economic rent. This is because of the short-term inflexibility of capital and increasing demand. In the long term, new capital innovation makes supply more elastic and reduces the rent element so only normal profits are made, i.e. profits cover factor costs.

Money and the Determination of the Rate of Interest

Money has different functions. It acts as a unit of account the unit in which prices are quoted. It acts as a store of value, although some currencies have performed much better than others in this respect. Its most important function is a medium of exchange, a means of payment for goods and services and in the settlement of debts.

Liquidity preference means that households and firms choose to hold money rather than other forms of assets: bonds, shares, paintings, etc. Keynes identified three motives for demanding or holding money.

- The transactions demand reflects the fact that the streams of income and expenditure seldom coincide, so that money is held in anticipation of being needed to pay for goods and services. The larger the value of transactions the larger the demand for money.

- The precautionary demand also depends mainly upon the value of transactions It differs from the transactions demand in that the transactions can be less clearly foreseen.

- Lastly, there is the speculative demand for money. The lower the yield on other assets, e.g,. the rate of interest on bonds, the higher the asset demand for money.

Together these three demands give the total demand for money. This varies inversely with the rate of interest (or more generally with the yield on other assets), as shown in figure 4.4. An increase in national income, i.e. value of transactions, causes the schedule to shift to the right from D1 to D2. If the money stock S is unchanged, this causes the equilibrium interest rate to increase from r1 to r2.

Fig. 4.4: Liquidity Preference Theory

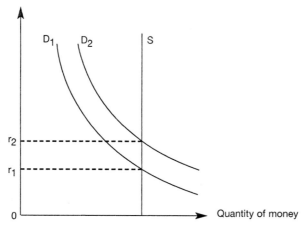

Another explanation of the determination of interest rates is provided by the *loanable funds theory.*

The rate of interest is the price at which money services are traded (borrowed and loaned). The higher the rate of interest the higher is the reward for deferring spending and therefore the higher the quantity of loanable funds supplied (figure 4.5). The higher the rate of interest the higher is the cost of being able to spend now rather than later, and therefore the smaller is the quantity of loanable funds demanded. The equilibrium rate of interest is that at which the quantity of loanable funds demanded equals the quantity supplied often by the same people but for different reasons.

The loanable funds theory shows the real interest rate, r2 in figure 4.5, reflecting the demand and supply of loanable funds. These funds are supplied and demanded by the same players, namely companies, individuals, governments and overseas speculators, at different times and for different reasons. Demand for loanable funds reflects:

- Investment opportunities and profitability.
- General government borrowing requirements.
- Speculative demand for exchange and interest rates.

Supply for loanable funds reflects:

- Inflationary pressures.
- Savings and profit levels.
- The risk from holding loanable funds rather than other assets.

Fig. 4.5: Loanable Funds Theory

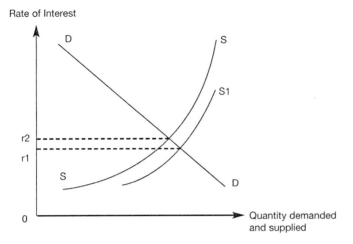

In the liquidity preference approach, if the demand for money is given, an increase in the money supply would cause the rate of interest to fall. In the loanable funds approach, an increase in the supply of money would cause an increase in the supply of loanable funds leading to a fall in the rate of interest. Conversely a fall in the supply of money would cause the interest rate to rise in both theories, i.e. r1 to r2. Interest rates could increase if government borrowing increases or inflationary pressures reduce savings.

The cost of capital and the level of investment

Companies seek finance by debt or by issuing shares. They expect to invest the money in projects, such as the building and new factories whose yield exceeds the cost of capital. In figure C, investment projects are ranked in accordance with the potential yield or rate of return i.e. profit. For example, projects requiring Q1 of finance have a potential rate of return of 6% or above. Further projects have lower rates of return, i.e. 4%.

If a project's yield could be guaranteed, it would be undertaken if the yield exceeded the cost of capital. In the uncertain world in which companies operate they may look for a safety margin so that, for example, Q2 investment would be undertaken at a cost of capital less than 4%.

Investment is financed partly by retained earnings, partly by borrowing and partly by issuing shares (equity capital). The overall cost of finance is the weighted average of these three sources. For example, if the (after tax) costs were: borrowing 5%; retained earnings 7%; equity capital 9%; and the same amount was raised from all three sources, the overall cost of finance would be 7%. ie 5 + 7 + 9 ÷ 3 = 7

Fig. C: The Cost of Capital and the Level of Investment

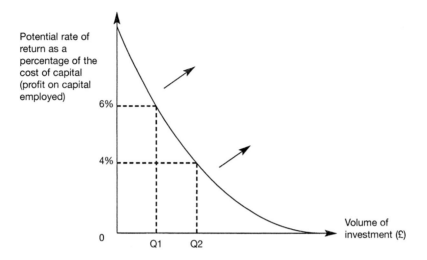

If the overall cost is 6%, then Q1 investment will be undertaken; cost equals the profit rate. If the cost falls to 4% more investment is undertaken i.e., Q2 . Improvements in technology improve profit potential on investment so the overall schedule shifts to the right so more investment to undertaken at all interest rates.

Data Response 1

Agricultural Property Prices

Newton Farm £1500 per acre	close to the Edinburgh-London railway and St. Andrews 494 acres trout loch, clay pigeon shoot, off road 4x4 driving course.
Cardwick £3,000 per acre	Tenanted Farm; 1st grade silt land: cereals and vegetables
Stream Farm £2,200 per acre	530 acres; hill farm with sheep and cattle
Bishopstoke £500 per acre	200+ acres; mixed farming, fishing lake stocked with Rainbow trout

Use supply and demand analysis to discuss why regional agricultural land prices vary.

Data Response 2

A region has two sectors: industrial and residential. The diagram shows their demand schedules (D1 and Dr), SS shows fixed supply of land.

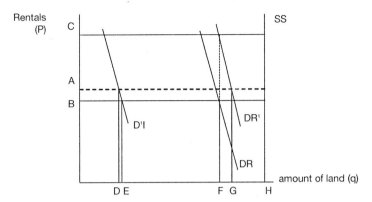

The government decides to subsidise house purchase and this shifts demand for residential land to DR1.

1. Given the equilibrium rental, show initial allocation of land.

2. After the subsidy has been given, show the rental rates in the sectors in the short run.

3. What will be the equilibrium position in the long run in term of (p/q) for both sectors?

4. Show the short-term gain in rental values to the landlords of residential land.

5. What will be the impact in the long run of the subsidy?

Data Response 3

The UK Labour Market

The labour market in this country is one of the most studied but probably least understood of all markets. There are a wide range of views about the nature of the labour market. On the one side there are the 'equilibrium theorists', who argue that the labour market is not dissimilar to competitive markets, like that for cabbages or foreign exchange. Thus the price in each market, be it cabbages or labour, is determined by the equality of supply and demand. Equilibrium theorists argue that real wages adjust quickly to changes in supply and demand.

An important part of the equilibrium approach is the explanation it suggests for the pattern of rising real wages and unemployment. The explanation advanced is couched in terms of upward (leftward) shifts in labour supply, these reductions in the supply of labour being the result of increases in the value of social security benefits and of increasing pressure on the labour markets by trade union activity. In an equilibrium model, measured unemployment is then explained by the rational supply decisions by workers, although it is also recognised that there will be frictional unemployment even in competitive labour markets. Such frictional unemployment is, of course, an almost inevitable feature of a flexible, changing economy, and as such is not evidence of problems in the labour market. In the main, the argument put forward by equilibrium theorists is a supply side explanation of changes in measured unemployment. Put another way, they argue that the natural or equilibrium rate of unemployment increased substantially during the 1980s largely due to these supply side effects.

The other or opposite view of the labour market is that it is more or less permanently in disequilibrium, with the supply of labour not being brought into equality with the demand, by smooth quickly adjusted real wages. According to this alternative, real wages are rigid, especially downwards. Hence a fall in the demand for labour, for example, will be reflected in an increase in unemployment, which is largely involuntary, and which will tend to persist.

'Disequilibrium theorists' generally advocate demand reflation as a means of reducing unemployment.

Source: Lloyds Bank Review, number 165.

1. Explain the similarities between the market for cabbages and the market for labour.

2. Use a diagram to explain the patterns of rising real wages and unemployment to the labour market.

3. Discuss the alternative policies to reduce unemployment likely to be advocated by the two groups of theorists in the passage.

Data Response 4a

Diagram A shows wage elasticity of demand for premier league footballers (f) and first class cricketers (c) in the UK. Diagram B shows long run income elasticity for premier league flootball (f) and first class cricket fixtures (c).

1. Discuss the impact of supply changes on wage levels in both sports.

2. Comment on the respective income elasticities shown and discuss how boom and slump affects industry income.

3. Outline the likely price elasticities of each sport and discuss the ways in which both sports could generate extra revenues.

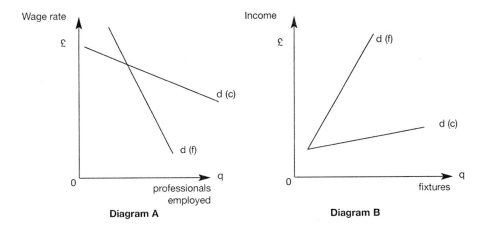

Diagram A   **Diagram B**

Data Response 4b

The Market for Business Studies Teachers

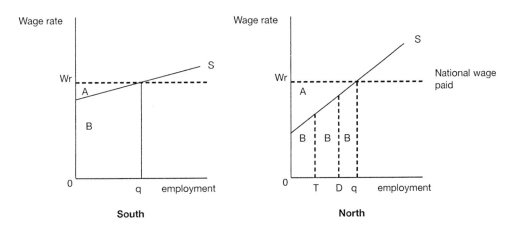

South   **North**

(Wr = same national wage)

It is often alleged that market conditions for different teachers vary in the North and South of England.

1. On what basis could the above diagrams be explained?

2. Identify the areas A and B and indicate what each diagram shows.

3. How might policy makers react to the above with regard to wage negotiations and taxation policy?

4. In the absence of a national wage T and D are paid, in the North, different wages. How can this occur? Who benefits?

Data Response 5

Non-Clearing Labour Markets

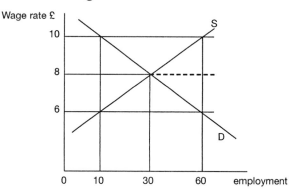

Which of the following could not maintain the wage level at £10?

    a. a minimum wage agreement

    b. a strong trade union agreement

    c. imperfectly competitive product markets

    d. expensive labour market recruitment

    e. a competitive labour market

    f. a £2 per unit tax on labour

    g. a £4 per unit subsidy on labour.

Data Response 6

Incentive effects

One of the justifications that is often given for cutting taxes is that it will increase the amount of work done in the economy.

The essence of the argument is that tax cuts allow people to retain a larger proportion of the reward they get for work so they will choose to supply more of it.

One problem in analysing this view is that there are many different aspects of work there is the length of time spend working in any given period, there is the amount of skill people acquire to bring to their work; there is the level of responsibility or risk people are prepared to accept in their jobs.

Let us begin with those already paying tax. An increase in the tax threshold simply presents everyone with the same extra amount, however much work they do, as long as they continue to do enough work to pay tax. It has no effect on the additional income people get for additional work. The natural response to this free handout is to make people feel they do not have to work quite so hard.

How would these same people respond to a cut in the basic rate of tax? On the one hand, the individual now retains more of any gross wage which makes the work seem more rewarding and so encourages people to supply more of it (substituting work for leisure). On the other hand, cutting taxes make people feel better off and this makes them work less hard. This is the income effect of the tax cut. The overall effect could go either way, but a cut in the basic rate of tax presents people with very different amounts depending on just how much they were earning prior to the tax cut. We might expect there to be a sizeable income effect for those with large incomes.

For those whose earnings are right on the tax threshold, typically married people working part-time, raising the tax threshold will mean they can now work more, earn more and still not pay tax.

For those who are unemployed the effects of tax cuts depend very much on the reasons for their unemployment. For those who choose not to work, any form of tax cut raises the net income available from work, and makes the decision to work more attractive. For those actively seeking work, the key is more likely to be the link between an proposed wage and any benefits received as an unemployed person. Changes to tax thresholds are more likely to act as an incentive here than changes in the tax rate. Finally, for those who see no work available for them, tax cuts will make no difference.

What evidence we have suggest that incentive effects are small. there are, however, many aspects on which we have no empirical evidence and very little theory.

The message of this article is not that incentives are unimportant, but simply that cutting the basic rate of tax or raising allowances are excessively crude instruments with which to influence them.

Source: adapted from David Ulph, 'Tax cuts - will they work?' *Economic Review*.

1. Explain the terms (i) tax threshold, (ii) basic rate of tax, (iii) incentive effects.

2. Outline the main types of people effected by tax cuts.

3. Discuss the concept of income and distribution effect within the context of the passage.

Labour Markets: Statistical Note

The Distribution of Income: Frequency Distribution and Lorenz Curves

Figure A shows the frequency distribution in percentage terms for manual employees, male and female. This illustrates how frequency distributions can vary and in both cases distributions are positively skewed with most workers earning low wages.

Fig. A: Distribution of Gross Weekly Earnings in GB

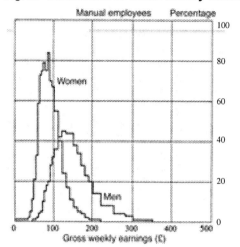

Lorenz Curves

The derivation of frequency distributions is based upon actual income received by householders. Another way of presenting this information is by a LORENZ CURVE. This indicates how far the actual distribution of income etc., deviates from a perfectly equal distribution. It is derived by calculating, in percentage terms, the cumulative change in both income and frequency variables. The further the curve is from the centre line the greater the inequality and vice versa. In the hypothetical Lorenz Curve figure B around 10% of pre-tax income earners receive 40% of income which illustrates how unequal income distribution often is. Lorenz Curves can be used to illustrate inequalities in other areas of economics, such as:

i.   Industrial concentration of output etc., over time etc.

ii.   Industrial output and costs (efficiency).

iii. The impact of taxation on incomes.

Fig. B: Lorenz Curve showing Hypothetical Pre and Post Tax Distribution of Income

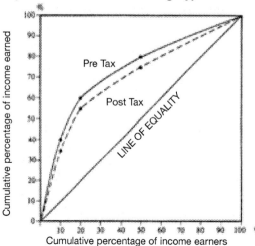

Distribution of Income in a
Hypothetical Economy

Income Share of	Pre Tax	Post Tax
Top 10%	40	35
Top 20%	60	55
Top 50%	80	75
Bottom 50%	20	25

chapter five
Market Failure
Government Intervention in Markets

Aims

To define, explain and discuss

- Pareto Optimum and Markets
- Market Failure and Weakness
- Remedies for Market Failure
- The Economics of Pollution

Key Concepts

Cost and Allocative Efficiency; Pareto Optimum; Externalities; Public Goods; Merit Goods; Marginal Costs of Pollution and Abatement; Pollution Quotas; Equality and Efficiency; Taxation (Regressive/Direct); Information Asymmetry

Governments and Markets - Micro Economic Policy

In order to understand why governments intervene in markets it is important to define economic efficiency. Economic efficiency, according to the Pareto definition (Pareto optimum) is the idea that, for a given range of demand tastes, resources and technology, it is impossible to move to another allocation which would make some people better off and nobody worse off, that is the economy has achieved the best possible distribution of goods. A Pareto Optimum is illustrated in figure 5.1. Here the present allocation is at z for both individuals A and B. Using the idea of a Pareto optimum, only points in region c guarantee an improvement for both A and B. In region b both are worse off whilst in regions a and d one is better off at the expense of the other. In economics a Pareto optimum also requires cost efficiency in order to ensure allocative efficiency (see figure 5.2). This shows that for productive or cost efficiency, marginal cost, for the firm, must be minimised at MC and not

Fig. 5.1 Pareto Optimum

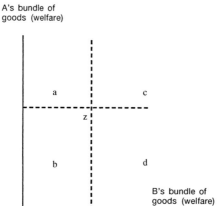

MC1. The shaded difference between the two could be due to monopolistic inefficiency or organisational slack. Furthermore the firm should also operate at the lowest point on its long-run average cost curve, LAC. Under monopolistic conditions, with excess capacity, the industry could be operating inefficiently at points a or c. Competition ensures an output of 0q which minimises costs at b and this, in the long run, will be where market demand equals supply.

Fig. 5.2 Productive/Allocative Efficiency: The Firm

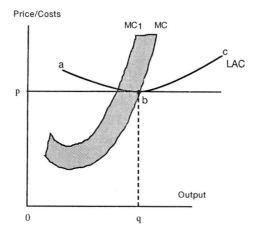

In a free market, economic efficiency is maximised if price equals both MC and LAC at b, since it also equals marginal utility; resources could not be reallocated without making someone worse off. Figure 5.3 shows the supply schedule as the sum of private marginal costs for firms whilst demand is the sum of private marginal utility or benefits for consumers. The long-run equilibrium for price and output is 0p/0q which is also at the lowest point on the long-run average cost curve LAC; it is a Pareto Optimum. Suppose the free market equilibrium were disturbed so the market moved to either output 0q1 or 0q2. At 0q1 marginal benefits (D) exceed marginal costs (S) so society would gain triangle a by moving to output 0q. At 0q2, MC exceeds MB so society would gain triangle b by moving to output 0q. Thus 0q is a Pareto Optimum.

Fig. 5.3 Productive/Allocative Efficiency: The Market

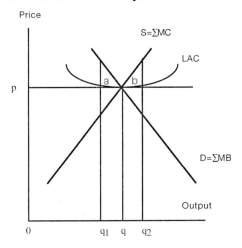

Consumer and Producer Surplus (Area Analysis)

Another approach illustrating the Pareto optimum is one which uses the idea of consumer and producer surpluses, (see figure 5.4). The area under the demand curve, at price 0p, reflects total benefits paid for (areas b plus c) plus consumer benefits not paid for (area a). The supply curve reflects resource costs at output 0q (area c) plus the producer's profits or surplus (area b). The free market optimum 0p/0q maximises the net benefits to the community. These net benefits are areas a plus b: consumer surpluses (a) and producer surpluses (b). Total net benefits cannot be improved upon at any other output level. This approach has been developed in 'area analysis' which is used to analyse comparative market situations.

Fig. 5.4 Consumer and Producer Benefits: Maximise Net Benefits

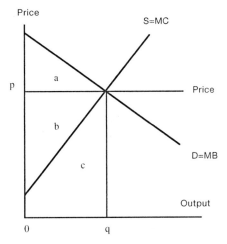

Advantages of Free Markets

The above analysis illustrates how the free market equilibrium, at 0p/0q:

- Maximises productive and allocative efficiency, that is achieves a Pareto optimum.

- Coordinates consumer and producer decisions without the need for conscious and expensive direction of a bureaucracy.

- Automatically relates price to private costs and benefits and so maximises social benefits.

- Directs resources to where marginal revenue equals marginal costs.

- Acts as an information system for both producers and consumers. Hayek argues that the free market is a discovery process whereby consumers signal their preferences to producers by price movements and resources are reallocated as these preferences are revealed in the market system. Government intervention can, says Hayek, often distort these signals and confuse producers and consumers.

Drawbacks of the Free Market

The free market's use of resources to achieve a Pareto optimum only works under certain conditions which are often unrealistic and which have to be corrected by government intervention. These qualifications are listed and discussed in detail below.

Perfectly Competitive Markets Absent

The existence of monopoly power, other things equal, causes output to fall and price to rise. Under perfect competition, where AR = MR, equilibrium output is q1 where MC = MR = AR and price is P1 in figure 5.5. Suppose that the industry becomes a monopoly. The monopolist can sell a greater output only by reducing the price and therefore faces a downward sloping AR curve with a diverging MR curve beneath it. Profit-maximising equilibrium output falls to q2 where MC = MR and price rises to p2. The extent to which social welfare fails to be maximised, that is, the extent to which resources are misallocated, is shown by the welfare triangles a and b, a representing the loss of consumers' surplus and b the loss of profit caused by the reduction in output from q1 to q2. There is no such thing as a perfectly competitive market in the real world and so in practice the free market economy fails to make the best use of resources to the extent that its constituent markets embody monopoly power. If, however, a monopoly leads to the attainment of economies of scale, the MC curve will move outwards and the efficiency gains will restore some of the output lost under monopoly. This shifts the MC downwards to MC1 which cuts MR at an output of 0q1 or beyond. In this case the monopolist can produce at an output level and at a price which is compatible with the free market one of 0p1 where MC = AR.

Fig. 5.5 Monopolistic and Competitive Equilibrium

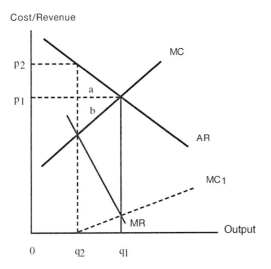

Public Goods

A pure public good exhibits, firstly, non-rivalry in consumption, as in the case of nuclear defence, where the supposed benefit to A of being protected from nuclear attack does not mean that there is less benefit left for B. The second characteristic of a pure public good is non-excludability: once the good is provided for A it is impossible to exclude B from its benefits. For example, providing a 'nuclear umbrella' for one person automatically affords equal protection to her neighbours. B will not pay towards providing a public good, because no rational agent will pay for benefits she is going to receive for nothing. When A sees that B is a 'free rider' she too will refuse to pay. Thus, the free market is incapable of providing public goods, despite the fact that society (both A and B in the example) would be better off with the good than without it. Street lighting and other local services are public goods and were paid for by local rates. It was alleged, however, that this system allowed some to use local services freely because rates were not paid by all who lived locally but only by house owners; they were 'free riders'. This was one reason why the community charge or 'poll tax' was introduced, because this had a broader tax base and so everyone over 18 years (with some exceptions) contributed to the financing of local services.

Merit/Demerit Goods

Merit goods are those goods the consumption of which is believed to be meritorious. Thus, a good might provide greater benefits to an individual than he/she herself realises. For example, it is considered to be in a child's own long-term interests to be compelled to attend primary school even if this is not apparent to the child herself, or perhaps to her parents. From this perspective, a free market, by responding to consumer preferences alone, would supply less than the optimal amount of primary schooling. The benefits of a child's education might accrue to other people as well as to the child herself, a possibility which raises the issue of externalities.

Demerit goods are those goods the consumption of which is considered, by the state, to be bad for the individual and society. Thus excessive smoking or drinking of alcohol is harmful and costly and these are demerit goods; they are bad for you. The state attempts to increase the consumption of merit goods, such as education and/or health, and reduce the consumption of demerit goods by using a mixture of taxation and subsidies as figure 5.6 illustrates. A free market solution is shown by price/output of 0p/0q. The government considers the good to be of merit and wishes to encourage consumption to 0q1; this is a Pareto optimum. This level can be achieved by (i) state provision of 0q1, by (ii) an advertising campaign increasing community awareness of the benefits of the good which then increases demand to D1, or by (iii) a subsidy, S to S2, which reduces the free market price to 0p1.

Fig. 5.6 Dealing With Merit/Demerit Goods

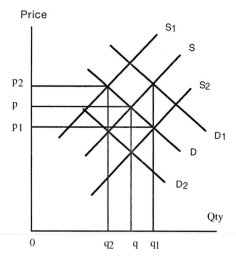

A demerit good can be similarly treated. A government wishes only 0q2 to be consumed. It may achieve this by (i) allowing only 0q2 on to the market, (ii) a tax could be placed on the good so shifting S to S1 and price rises to 0p2. Alternatively an advertising campaign, warning of the dangers of the product, could reduce demand to D2. In effect by providing more information of the merits or demerits of the good the individual is made aware of the true value of the good through the market system. The role of the government in this is to provide the correct information.

Price Instability in Markets

Many agricultural and raw material markets are characterised by price and income instability. This is due to (i) poor market information by suppliers, (ii) a time lag between recognising a demand change and being able to provide for it and (iii) because forward output planning is difficult due to poor market operation. The result of price volatility is that producers have an uncertain income and forward investment in future output is patchy. uncertain and inadequate. The role of government under these circumstances is to stabilise markets by supporting farmers' incomes or market price. (See Chapter 3).

Risk or Uncertainty

Many markets are characterised by risk and uncertainty with regard to the future. Whilst insurance and other contingency techniques have reduced this risk, many markets still suffer from product uncertainty due to moral hazard or adverse selection. Furthermore, when forward markets are unavailable then consumers cannot make their future preferences known. As many futures markets do not exist and because risk can reduce output below the Pareto optimum then inefficiency increases. The role of the government in these circumstances is to encourage markets to develop by covering possible losses as in the case of overseas trade risk, for example ECGD. Governments can also provide health provision, such as care for the elderly, which could not be adequately provided by the private sector due to problems of adverse selection within the insurance markets.

Information Problems - Asymmetry

Because of moral hazard and adverse selection problems, consumers and producers may know more than each other (asymmetry) so they may never trust the market price as an indicator of benefits or production costs. In financial markets consumers may not be fully aware of product safety, quality or reliability and in financial markets 'insider trader' dealings can increase consumer distrust in capital markets. Providers of insurance may find, because of moral hazard and adverse selection problems, actual provision costs greatly exceed budgeted costs which may lead them to withdraw from markets; markets will then operate inefficiently. Efficient markets are those where all possible information is equally and readily available to producers and consumers and so the role of the government is to ensure this condition applies. This would lead governments to insist, to both consumers and producers, upon full disclosure of relevant information with regard to the safety, producer quality and risk aspects of goods and services. This will encourage consumers and producers to re-enter the market. 'Insider trader' dealings help improve the efficiency of a market by providing an incentive to look for information but it is illegal because it is not fairly available to all !

Fig. 5.7 Positive Externalities (Benefits)

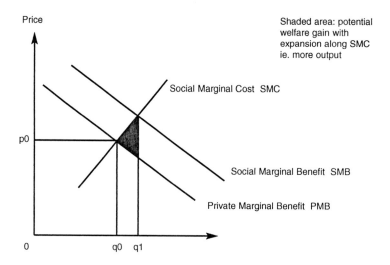

Externalities in Consumption or Production

The free market equilibrium assumes all the costs and benefits are private and internal to the market. In reality there are benefits other than those paid for by the consumer. These can be in consumption or production. When I telephone a person the phone call provides benefits which are not paid for directly by the receiver of the call. In production I can benefit from the crop spraying of my neighbouring farmer. There can also be additional costs incurred when others consume or produce. When I smoke cigarettes others suffer from the fumes whilst the production of cement or bricks means others have clear up costs incurred upon them. These extra benefits or costs are external to the market and are known as externalities. The free market will supply less than the socially optimal quantity of a good providing external benefits. Individual consumers demand only 0q at a price of 0p which reflects only the private benefits of the good to each consumer (see fig. 5.7). The external benefits push society's demand curve out to MB1, and the socially optimal output is 0q1. For example, A's vaccination against a contagious disease benefits B, who might have caught the disease from A if A had remained unvaccinated. Conversely, the free market will supply more than the socially optimal quantity of a good with external costs. Adding these negative externalities to the costs of production shifts the MC curve backwards to MC1 and shows that the socially optimal output is 0q1 rather than 0q (see fig. 5.8). Pollution and other damage to the environment are obvious external costs of free market transactions. The net benefits and losses of increasing and decreasing outputs in each case are shown by the shaded triangles. These are net gains in 5.7 and net losses in 5.8.

Fig. 5.8 Negative Externalities (Costs)

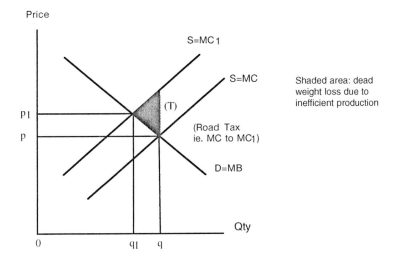

Dealing with Externalities

The following identify methods of dealing with and correcting externalities.

Government's Tax or Subsidise

As discussed above, governments can discourage production or consumption by taxation (T) aimed at reflecting social costs or can subsidise (S) production or consumption in order to acknowledge and encourage benefits.

Grant Legal Property Rights - Compensation

The government or the common law can assign to consumers or producers certain legal 'rights', such as the right to clean air, etc. If these rights are violated by the polluter, the consumer can sue the producer. In theory the compensation claimed should be the same as the tax imposed so pollution reduces by the amount shown in figure 5.8. A cheaper, non-legal solution may be for the polluting company to pay compensation to the victim/s of the pollution. Even if rights are not granted it is alleged that the cheapest solution is to allow those affected by the pollution to meet with the polluter and come to an economic bargaining solution. This means either the polluter pays compensation or those being polluted pay the polluter to stop polluting. Thus the social costs are 'internalised' by the market. This is known as the 'Coase' solution. However, for this to be a practical solution those being affected have to organise themselves into a force able to take on a large corporation doing the polluting. The risk of expensive legal action together with 'free rider' problems on the part of some affected consumers means in practice that consumer groups may not press fully for the optimum solution because of the transaction costs involved.

Direct Controls or Standards

Governments have sought to limit pollution and other negative externalities imposed on the individual or society by setting controls on emission of pollution and/or by setting industry standards for pollution and/or behaviour. The former idea applies to toxic chemical wastes and the latter applies to such problems as noise levels, smoke emissions and the behaviour of media advertising, for example there are controls on advertising alcoholic drink on the television. These rules and regulations normally apply across an industry or sector and can be enforced by a state-financed regulatory agency.

Using the Market to Clear Up External Costs

This approach used in the USA is now seen as a serious alternative to the above techniques. As reported in the *Economist* of 8th September 1990:

> In America some of the more far-sighted green lobbying groups have been helping to devise ways to work with the market, rather than against it. America's new clean-air legislation, based on ideas developed by the Environmental Defence Fund (EDF), sets an absolute cap on emissions of sulphur dioxide and nitrous oxide by power stations. It then gives companies permits to emit a certain amount of the gases each year, and allows them to buy or sell these permits. The aim is to encourage those power stations which can clean up most cheaply to do so, and then make money by selling spare polluting capacity to those for whom cleaning up is expensive.

> Already, this potential new market is attracting a new kind of trader who will help to make it work more efficiently. Mr. John Palmisano, whose company ALR*X has been arranging trades in pollution permits under an older, less satisfactory bit of clean-air legislation, looks forward to a big increase in business. He is the only specialised broker in the business. Since the new clean-air bill came before Congress, others have become interested: for instance, Asea Brown Boveri, a European engineering firm, has recently bought Combustion Engineering, the largest manufacturer of scrubbers in America. A growing number of companies are putting together broking skills, engineering expertise and an understanding of environmental regulations. They will then approach companies, offering to cut their

emissions and pay for it by selling their spare emission rights. 'My best client is the finance manager,' says Mr. Palmisano. 'Not the pollution-control manager, who is probably an engineer with a strong not-invented-here attitude.

However, some economists argue that tradeable licences to pollute act as an entry barrier (cost) for would-be entrants into the industry since incumbents own the licences to pollute.

Furthermore, trading companies, rather than governments or taxpayers, make profits by selling these licences to those who will still pollute as they come into the industry.

An optimum level for pollution

Economic theory shows that to be efficient the polluter (firm, individual or government) should pay the full cost of environmental damage caused by its activity. This would create an incentive for the reduction of such damage. to the level where the marginal cost of pollution reduction is equal to the marginal cost of damage caused by such pollution.

Fig 5.9: The Economic Optimum Level of Pollution

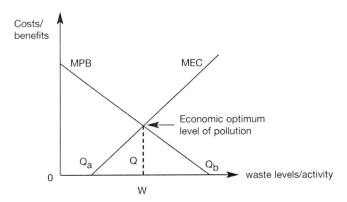

In figure 5.9, a firm's activity level Q and related levels of waste W are shown on the horizontal axis. It is assumed that, at any level below activity level Qa. the waste can be absorbed by the environment. Any external cost is temporary (contamination but not permanent pollution).

The extra benefit received by a polluting firm from increasing its activity by one unit is shown by the marginal private benefit curve MPB. The value of the extra economic damage done by the pollution from each extra unit is shown by the marginal external cost curve MEC. The optimum level of pollution is then determined by the intersection of the two curves where the activity level would be at Q and waste at W.

Property Rights and Coase's Theory (Post A level)

Coase's theory, developed in the 1960s emphasises the importance of property rights and bargaining between polluters and those suffering from the pollution. Coase argued that polluter and sufferers should be left in an unregulated situation where a bargaining process would develop. An agreement would be reached which would reflect the power of each party in relation to ownership of property rights. There would be an automatic move towards the social optimum through the bargaining process.

Left unregulated, the polluter will try to operate at the level of activity at which its returns are maximise - at which point marginal private benefits (the extra benefits accrued by the polluter for each additional unit of activity) fall to zero. This is shown in figure 5.9b as level Qp. However, the social optimum is at Qs where returns are balanced by the full external costs of pollution.

If the sufferer has property rights, then it benefits the polluter to compensate the sufferer up to the level Qs. Beyond Qs, the sufferer's losses are greater than the polluter's gains. If the property rights belong to the polluter, the analysis starts at Qp with the sufferer given the opportunity to compensate the polluter. The tendency is to move towards level Qs, the social optimum.

Many reservations have been express about the theory. There may be difficulties in identifying the polluter and the sufferer; there may be high transaction costs, especially if lawyers are involved; and it surely matters a great deal in practice who holds the property rights in question. There are extreme situations where the rights are clear. Landowners, for example, do not have the right to dump hazardous chemicals in streams and rivers. They do not have the right to select the mix of capital and labour to use on their land. In between comes a whole range of situations (loss of wetlands as the result of drainage, application of fertilisers, etc.) where there are likely to be disputes over property rights.

Government Provision - Cost Benefit Analysis

In many sectors social benefits far outweigh social costs but the private sector fails to recognise this and so it underinvests in the provision of the goods, for example roads, etc. Cost Benefit Analysis (CBA) in such public investment projects identifies and attempts to value social costs and benefits in order that a comprehensive comparison of private and social costs and benefits can be evaluated. Cost Benefit Analysis of the MI motorway, the Victoria underground line in London, and the Severn Bridge all provided evidence that the value of discounted social benefits exceeded the private and social costs of constructing and operating these large civil engineering projects. This analysis helped governments evaluate and publicly fund major infrastructure projects in the 1970s, although the cutbacks in public investment in the 1980s reduced the importance of CBA. The Channel Tunnel link between the UK and France was privately funded, on the UK side, and its operation has been a private venture. Public investment in this project, aided by CBA, may have been able to fully appreciate both micro- and macro-social benefits.

Fig. 5.9b

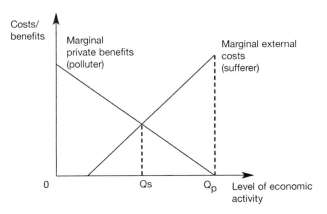

Subsidy to Polluter

Where constant pollution occurs due, say, to a faulty machine, a last chance solution might be to pay the polluter a subsidy to replace the machine and remove all pollution.

Dealing with Externalities - the Cement Production Case

Figure 5.10 illustrates both private and social costs of pollution caused by a cement works together with marginal clean-up costs. The vertical axis measures the costs whilst the horizontal axis at zero shows no pollution and moves to high pollution emission of around 400 units. As pollution increases the marginal cost to the firm increases as machines become more difficult to operate and dirt and pollution affect the neighbourhood, that is social pollution costs increase. There are a number of achievable levels of pollution together with remedy policies which could be used. These are outlined as follows.

The Green Solution of Zero Pollution

Corresponding to output level (a), this is an ideal solution but the cost of clean up is far in excess of the damage to society and the firm. Thus the high clean up costs outweigh any gains in benefits and the resources used to clean up pollution could be used more efficiently, in terms of potential benefits, elsewhere.

The Unregulated and the Social Optimum Output

The unregulated approach to pollution would rely upon the producer to reduce pollution up to the level (b) where the marginal private damage to the firm equals the marginal cost of clean up. However, this level means that the social costs of pollution are ignored. When these are taken into account the optimum level of pollution emission is at level (c), 130 units, which corresponds with both clean up costs and pollution damage of around £25th. At this level of pollution (c) there is around £10th worth of private pollution and £15th worth of social pollution. This is a Pareto optimum but the problem is how best can this level be achieved ? The following policies outline a range of solutions.

Fig. 5.10 Dealing with Pollution: Cement

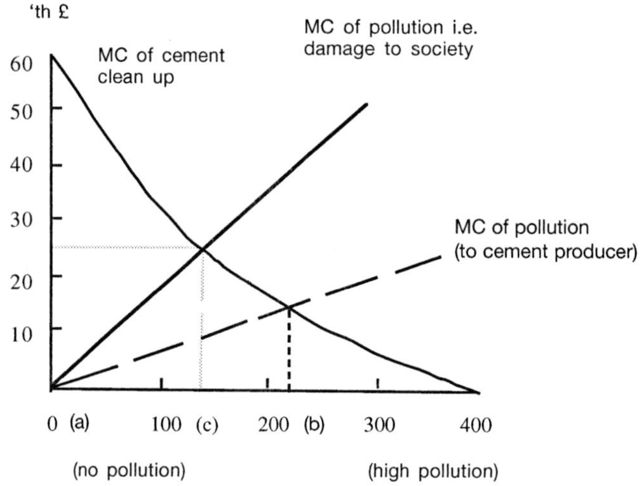

Grant Legal Property Rights to Those Affected

If those affected could be given the right not to be polluted then they could sue for compensation, ideally up to £10th representing the private pollution caused. However, there are practical problems. Those affected may rely on others to take action and the legal costs may deter action so that a second best solution between b and c may result.

Direct Controls by Government Pollution Agencies

If the government set standards of pollution emission which can be enforced by imposing fines upon the polluters then in theory the optimum level (c) can be attained. However, if the level of fines is low then the cement works could flout these standards. Furthermore, direct standards of control fail to appreciate that the marginal costs of clean up vary between cement works so there is no financial incentive to clean up for the firm other than the fines imposed.

Emission Taxes and Pollution

This policy attempts to theoretically graduate taxation imposed on the cement works and is equivalent to the difference between the marginal cost to the firm and to society, with respect to pollution caused. It would be equivalent to £l5th at c. However, in practice there is the problem of correctly estimating the amount of tax for both the cement works and/or the industry. Also the enforcement costs of tax collecting could outweigh any extra benefits gained.

Using the Market to Reduce Pollution

Assume that figure 5.10 illustrates the whole cement industry then the market solution would be to allow so much pollution, 130 units at c, and this amount of pollution is rationed between cement works in the industry, and each works is allowed to emit so much pollution. This means low-cost, clean-up cement works are given the same pollution allowances as high-cost, clean-up works. The low-cost works can attain their levels of pollution limits and then sell for a profit some of their unused pollution quotas to high-cost clean up firms. This means there will be a built-in incentive to clean-up since unused pollution rations can be sold for a profit. Furthermore, the bureaucracy costs of tax collection and setting up legally enforceable standards of pollution emission are eliminated. Proponents of this market solution allege there is a built-in incentive to reduce clean-up costs. In effect this shifts the MC of cement clean up to the left and so a lower social optimum of pollution is achieved at no extra costs to the community. On the other hand, it is alleged that incumbents who have been granted these emission quotas may well use them as barriers to entry for new would-be cement works.

Efficiency and Equality - the Impact of Taxation on Markets

Governments use taxation and subsidies in order to achieve the two conflicting objectives of economic efficiency and equality of income. Income tax policies, designed to reduce inequality of income, and/or regional subsidies, designed to boost employment, are, it is alleged, economically inefficient since they distort prices and ensure that they are never equated to marginal cost, that is market forces are not allowed to operate.

Equality and Progressive Taxation

Taxation policies use the concept of (i) direct/indirect tax and (ii) progressive/regressive tax. A direct tax is one which is directly placed upon expenditure, such as VAT, because this directly taxes income. A progressive tax is one where the percentage of tax paid either directly or indirectly from income rises, whilst a regressive one has the opposite effect. A proportional tax takes a constant proportion of income, for example corporation profits tax. These are illustrated in figure 5.11, viz. a, b and c. In each case for a, b and c the actual amount of tax paid can still increase; it is the percentage of income the tax represents which defines whether it is progressive, etc. The impact of a progressive, proportional and regressive tax are shown in figure 5.11 as a, b and c respectively.

Fig. 5.11   Progressive, Regressive and Proportional Taxation

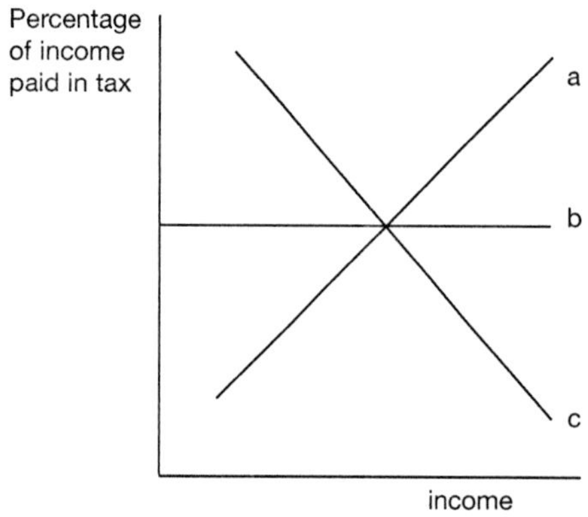

Finally table 5.1 shows a summary of why markets fail, the type of government remedy used and their effectiveness

Market failure and government remedies

Cause	Correction	Effectiveness = Politics
Time-lag	Supply-side policy	Do incentives work?
	Deregulation	Imperfect information
Unequal distribution of income	Progressive income tax	Does the right group benefit?
	Transfer payments	Who decides?
	Maximum price legislation	
	Merit goods	
Producer power eg monopoly	Competition policy	Assessment problems
	Privatisation	Enforcement problems
Externalities eg social costs	Tax	Measurement problems
	Legislation	Enforcement problems
	Cost Benefit	Political
	Subsidy	
Free-rider problem	Public goods	Tax burden, limits

Source: Adapted

Data Response 1

The Regulation of Privatised Industries

Big profits mean bad regulation. Or so you would think from the outcry that greeted British Telecom's announcement that its profits in 1990-91 were £31.1 billion, which is equivalent to £97 per second. Much of the current uproar is due to a simple confusion between big, which the monopoly's profits certainly are, and too big. BT is Britain's biggest, most valuable and most profitable firm. but its profits are a relatively small proportion of sales (at 21.5%) and of capital (21.3%).

Even so, some of the privatised monopoly's profits may well be too high. The regulators certainly think so. Their main method of control is the pricing formula known as 'RPI minus X'. This means that each firm must limit its product price rises to 'X' percentage points less than the rate of inflation. If the regulator reckons that a firm is earning too much monopoly profit, it can raise 'X'. So far, the regulators have raised 'X' each time they have reviewed it.

This is no surprise. To get public sector managers to agree to be privatised, and to persuade investors to buy the shares, the Government had to offer incentives to the newly-privatised companies. In the case of the water companies, managers were encouraged to believe that they would be able to raise their prices to cover the costs of almost any investment. Once privatised, the Government has little reason to preserve such a friendly policy and every reason to make life tougher since consumers are voters.

'RPI means X' can work if the regulator has a good idea of how efficient the firm is, and how much better it could be. This is most likely when technology is fairly mature, so that the rate at which the regulators learn about the firm is faster than the rate at which the firm changes. In most of Britain's regulated monopolies, technology changes slowly as with gas pipes, water pipes, runways and so on. The big exception is telecommunications, where technology is changing fast.

Promoting competition should be the aim of the regulators, even in technologically mature industries. Britain still lacks a clear policy on vertical integration. Electricity has been broken into competitive generation and monopoly distributors, but gas and telecommunications remain more integrated. 'Yardstick' competition - comparing the performance of one local monopoly with other similar monopolies - has been considered by the regulators for some time, but it has still to be taken seriously used. 'Unbundling' the costs and prices of all a firm's activities - as BT began to do when it charged for directory enquiries and cut ordinary call charges - reduces unnecessary regulation and should go much further.

(Adapted from: 'The Role of the Regulators', in *The Economist*)

1. Discuss the factors that a regulator might take into account when deciding whether or not the profits made by a utility such as BT or a water company are too high.

2. Using the example of either gas or telecommunications, explain and illustrate the

term 'vertical integration' (line 25).

3. Discuss the advantages and disadvantages of breaking up the electricity industry into separate companies for generating and distributing electricity.

4. Identify how it is possible to 'promote' competition within an industry.

5. Are there any drawbacks to too much competition?

Data Response 2

Marginal Cost of Pollution and Marginal Cost of Pollution Control of a Cement Works

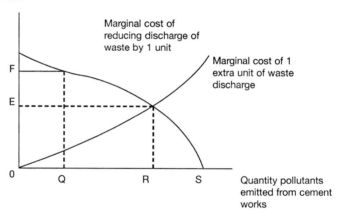

Identify the following statements with F, E,Q,R and S.

a.   the economically efficient output level

b.   the profit maximising businessman's output

c. the efficient marginal cost level

e. the likely 'Greenpeace' optimum output.

Data Response 3

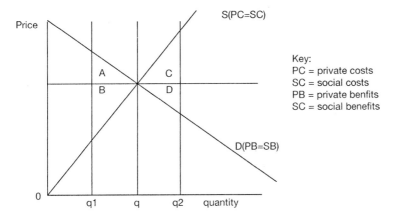

Key:
PC = private costs
SC = social costs
PB = private benfits
SC = social benefits

The free market equilibrium in the market is op/oq but a tax on the good reduces the amount bought and sold to 0q1 whilst a subsidy increases it to 0q2.

1. Use 'area' analysis to show that A + B are net losses to the community when a tax is imposed on a good or, e.g. on a free market wage.

2. Use an area analysis to show that C + D are net losses to the community when a subsidy is given on a good.

3. Under what conditions are social costs and benefits not same as private costs and benefits? Give examples.

4. Use the diagram to show that under certain circumstances areas A + B and C + D may be net gains to the community.

Data Response 4

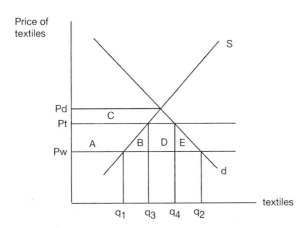

A country produces its own textiles in the absence of trade (pd). World imports are allowed in at Pw but a tariff is eventually placed upon the world price (Pt).

1. Identify the areas A, B, C, D and E.

2. Discuss the impact of the tariff on Pw.

3. What does the distance q2 less q represent?

Data Response 5

Case Study: The Econ Golf Club

The Econ Golf Club with 20 resident members, keeps a refrigerator stocked with beer. Each can of beer is obtained from a local distributor for 50 pence per can. Each member has free access to the refrigerator and can consume as many cans of soda or beer as he likes. At the end of each month, the total cost of the beer is divided evenly among the members.

1. If one member of the club drinks a can of beer, what is its cost to him?

2. What is the cost of this beer to the rest of the members of the club?

3. From the point of view of the club, what is the total social cost of the beer?

4. Is the amount of beer consumed by the club's members likely to depart from the amount that is socially efficient? If so, why?

5. What would be the social advantages and disadvantages of having each member buy and store his own beer.

6. What would be the social advantages and disadvantages of having a bartender with a key to the refrigerator who will open it during certain hours and sell beer at 50 pence per can?

7. What would be the social advantages and disadvantages of having the refrigerator open and asking each member to sign on a sheet (and later pay) for each can of beer he consumes?

8. If the Econ Golf Club contained 400 resident members, rather than 20, do you think that the relative advantages and disadvantages of these and other ways of handling this problem would be unaffected?

Data Response 6

Economics of a Lighthouse

A lighthouse warns fishing boats away from a rock. Different levels of service can be provided by the lighthouse, resulting in different probabilities that a boat will be warned of its nearness to the rock. For example, the more powerful the beacon or signal emitted by the lighthouse, the higher the probability that a boat will receive the warning. The marginal cost of attaining various probabilities that a boat will be warned is as shown in the graph below. There are three boats in the area, owned by X, Y and Z. The price that each captain is willing to pay for each level of service is shown by the individual demand curves in Figure A .

1. Is the service provided by the lighthouse a public good?

2. At the efficient level of service explain how free rider problems could arise.

3. Is it possible for a lighthouse to be privately owned and operated?

4. Show the aggregate demand schedule if the product were not a public good, i.e. a private good.

Fig. A

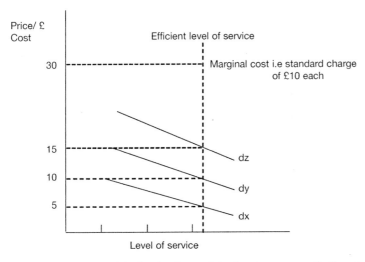

5. Compare the individual valuations of the boat owners with the standard charge of £10 each.

Data Response 7

A Liberalised Coal Market

The case for liberalisation begins from the argument that there is no obvious economic reason for centralising the British coal industry in one corporation. The industry is not a natural monopoly, where efficiency dictates that there should be only one supplier. Parts of some of the other fuel industries do have natural monopoly elements - for instance, long distance transmission and local distribution networks for electricity and gas. In such circumstances, there is a case for regulation (of which state ownership is one example) so that consumers are not exploited. but coal is a naturally competitive industry. Coal deposits are dispersed by nature, they vary in terms of size, quality and capital requirements. The natural state of the industry is one in which there are competing suppliers, though efficiency considerations would probably prevent there being separate ownership of each deposit. The essence of liberalisation is increased competition. It must therefore be distinguished clearly from some of the privatisation practised by the present government, which has involved no liberalisation at all but the mere transfer of monopolies from public to private sector. Privatisation British Gas - style is little, if any, advance on continued nationalised ownership.

Source: *Lloyds Bank Review*.

1. Explain what is meant by natural monopoly and say why efficiency dictates that there should be only one supplier. Give examples.

2. Use economic analysis to show the impact of a liberalisation policy upon the National Coal Board.

3. Explain what is meant by the last two sentences.

Data Response 8

Externalities on the Roads

Each morning, thousands of motorists travel the route from London's suburbs to the central business district where they work. Suppose that the full cost of this car trip - including both the money costs (of fuel, oil, tyre wear, and so on) and the value of the driver's (and passengers') time - is measured along the vertical axis of the graph below, and that the number of vehicles attempting this trip between 8.00 am and 9.00 am on a particular day is measured along the horizontal axis. The relationship between the full cost of this trip to a motorist and the number of vehicles attempting this trip is CC. The demand curve shows at each price of this trip (including both money and time costs) the number of vehicles that will set out on this route.

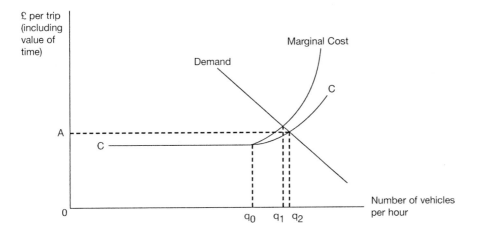

a   If more than Oqo vehicles attempt this trip, the cost of the trip increases as more and more vehicles per hour set out on this route. Why?

b   How many cars per hour will travel along this route?

c   Is this economically efficient number?

d   What measures might be taken to push the actual number closer to the efficient number?

Data Response 9

The following graph indicates the impact of social marginal benefits on the market for Underground Travel, e.g. London Transport.

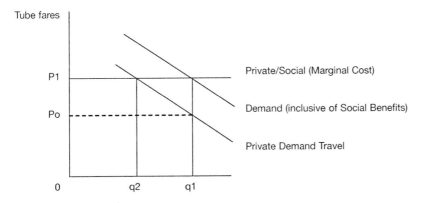

Which of the following statements is/are implied by the diagram?

a.   costs are zero whilst external benefits are positive

b.   economic efficiency is achieved with a subsidy of 0p1-0po.

Data Response 10

In the diagram π is the marginal profit derived by a firm from successive units of output.

E indicates the external cost in the form of pollution inflicted on the rest of society by successive units of output.

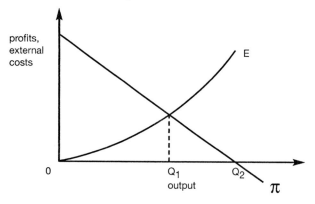

In the absence of negotiations between the affected parties, which outputs will be produced in the circumstances indicated in the table?

	firm has a legal right to pollute	public has a legal right to prevent pollution
A	OQ_1	OQ_1
B	OQ_1	OQ_2
C	OQ_2	zero
D	OQ_2	OQ_2
E	OQ_2	OQ_1

Data Response 11

What a load of old rubbish!

The recycling of products can lead to the recovery of natural resources that would otherwise have been wasted but recycling also creates new problems. All over Germany lie mountains of rubbish which no-one seems to be willing to turn into something else. Much of the problem stems from the fact that the collection side of recycling has been too successful. Germans have simply overstuffed their yellow rubbish bins and the over-supply is now rotting uselessly.

Recycling itself is also an expensive industrial process, consuming energy, involving transport costs and producing waste. Take galss for example, one of the most difficult materials to recycle, despite the popularity of bottle banks. If a household recycled 52 bottles a year, this would save about 6.2kg of carbon, but these savings would soon be lost if people drove to the bottle bank. Installing a low energy lighting in the home, for example, is over 200 times more effective than recycling. If paper is recycled more than three of four times, the fibres become too short to use for newspapers.

Source: adapted from *The Observer*, 28 July 1996

   and *Financial Times*, 28 November 1994

Making use of the information in the extract above and your knowledge of economics, discuss the reasons why the recycling of waste products may do little to help conserve the world's natural resources.

Data Response 12

Stop Rail Subsidies

The Majority pay for a rich elite to use this archaic form of travel

Even when you strip away double counting and exaggeration, present and projected subsidies to rail travel amount to tens of billions over a few years while three quarters of the cost of road travel, especially in private car, is taxation. Does this make sense in terms of economic logic or social justice?

In spite of its heavy subsidies, overt and covert, albeit euphemised as "investment", and the heavy tax burden on road travel, rail accounts for 8% of passengers; buses and coaches account for another 8%; while 84% is made up by the private car, hire car and taxi. The 8% of rail passengers for the most part represent the better-off people in the better-off parts of the country – over half of them are in the London Metropolitan region and 90% of taxpayers do not set foot in a train during the course of a year, but they foot the bill.

A side effect of heavy subsidies to rail travel is over concentration in central London and its vicinity, raising costs to local government subsidised by the Exchequer. Rail benefits from nearly 90% of dedicated track for its 8% of passenger mileage. Much of this subsidy could be better used to ease the cost burden to road users.

From the environmental standpoint, rail is extremely energy intensive, absorbing more than five times that needed for road travel, per passenger mile or ton mile, partly because of the great weight of metal carried and partly because electric traction is inherently more energy absorbent than the internal combustion engine. Fossil fuel at best retains a third of its value when converted to electricity; it moves great distances to reach the point of use at a high voltage and is converted to a much lower operating voltage at that point. This is particularly significant for rail.

Investment in rail provision is correspondingly more costly than road, with large amounts going on rails and signalling. Rail is less flexible as a form of transport than road: most rail travel is radial and many rail journeys begin and end by road. By the logic of travel, even heavy subsidies do little more than preserve rail's 8% share, since car ownership and use continue to expand by several per cent annually commensurate with population and income. Car travel suits light or heavy densities of road use and goes door to door.

One has to ask why the hue and cry for rail subsidies is so insistent while the 84% of car travel has so few defenders. This is partly a matter of social structure: the 8% of passenger miles by rail represents the metropolitan elite, and socio intellectual conservatism. The car age is new.

The car only began to come into its own in the 60's. In the 1955 traffic survey, rail still accounted for 40% of passenger mileage and buses 40%. The car was a middle-class perk. The masses travelled by bus or bike. Mindsets have yet to catch up with changing reality.

A few per cent of vested interests still determine the balance in transport – as they do in education and health. There seems to be a political disequilibrium too. The home counties commuters seem designed for the television news, whereas the car-using masses dispersed all over the country go unrecognised. Mindsets still see the car as a middle-class adjunct.

Here at least is an area in which the government can modernise at no cost, using the universal principle that you get what you pay for and pay for what you get. By and large, leaving aside really expensive districts in central London, the further you commute the higher your income will be. Transport subsidies mirror this. For modernisation is not confined to investment in machinery and fixed assets but entails rethinking yesterday's ideas. Steam has gone, but its intellectual constraints outlive it.

The question will be asked whether reform is politically possible. The answer is that the government is financially over-committed and will have to shed loads over the next few years. It is committed to spending much more on education and health, those great sponges soaking up money, which are closely monitored by the media and various interest groups. The eldorado of matching European levels of health expenditure may require the government to take voters into its confidence and leave the armies of disgruntled commuters to pay and grumble.

Alfred Sherman Guardian Newspaper Friday 18 January 2002

1. With reference to the above, discuss the economic arguments against rail subsidisation.

2. Discuss the argument that rail subsidisation could be considered to be a form of regressive taxation.

3. What are the implications of rail subsidisation for other forms of public expenditure?

chapter six

Costs, Revenue and the Output of the Competitive Market

Aims

To define, explain and discuss

- The Nature and Behaviour of Costs
- Costs and Output Decisions for the Firm
- Short Run and Long Run Decisions
- Scale Economics
- Market Structure and Costs
- Business Behaviour under Competitive Conditions
- The Influence of the Short and Long Run in Competitive Markets
- The Firm and Industry Equilibrium

Key Concepts

Fixed, Variable, Average and Marginal costs; Capacity and Optimum Output; Normal and Abnormal Profit; Long Run Envelope Curve; Economies and Diseconomies of Scale; Minimum Scale of Efficiency; Competitive Conditions; Price Taker, Short and Long Run Supply; Equilibrium

General Assumptions

In the long run the business unit exists in order to maximise profits, to total revenue (TR) less total cost (TC) equals maximum profit, for some level of output. This profit is defined as abnormal profits or economic rent and is different to normal profit. Normal profit includes an imputed cost element in terms of what factor inputs could have earned in the next best use. For example if capital could earn at least 10% interest in the bank, then total capital costs included this interest element. The theory of the economic business unit (the firm) assumes initially that those who manage the firm also own it so there is wholehearted support for the profit-maximising objective. There is no conflict of interest between managers and owners, that is no divorce of ownership and control, though in the shortterm non-profit maximising objectives, such as corporate growth, can be pursued in order to ensure maximum long-term profit. The last assumption is that the short run cost behaviour reflects diminishing return; costs are U-shaped though in the long run costs can rise, decrease or remain constant depending upon market conditions. This cost assumption is amended in certain examples.

Types of Behaviour of Costs

Types of Costs

Total costs (TC) are split into total variable (TVC) and total fixed costs (TFC). Variable costs depend upon output, for example there are direct or prime costs such as labour, materials or energy, etc. Fixed costs have to be paid regardless of output, for example rent, rates, interest charges, etc. In the short term, since these costs have often been paid, the firm can, under some circumstances, regard them as having no alternative use, that is zero opportunity cost, and so they may not have to be covered. This has led to the notion of 'let bygones be bygones' for short-run fixed costs. In the long run all costs have to be covered because fixed costs become variable.

Costs can also be defined as :

(i) Average fixed cost (AFC)   = $\dfrac{\text{Total fixed costs (TFC)}}{\text{output (n)}}$

(ii) Average variable costs (AVC)   = $\dfrac{\text{Total variable costs (TVC)}}{\text{output (n)}}$

(iii) Average total costs (ATC)   = $\dfrac{\text{Total costs} = \text{unit costs}}{\text{output (n)}}$

Note: (I) + (ii) = (iii), output (n) can be for the number of widgets produced, air miles covered, haircuts, theatre seats, insurance premiums sold, patients treated, etc.

The Behaviour of Costs

Figure 6.1 (a-d) illustrates the behaviour of costs. The behaviour of total costs (a) indicates that TFC is constant over some output range and TVC rises reflecting diminishing returns. The behaviour of TC reflects how marginal cost (MC) changes see below.

Figure 6.1 (b) shows average fixed costs fall rapidly as overheads are initially spread over more and more units of output, for example 100 ÷ 1 = 100, 100 ÷ 2 = 50, etc. but unit fixed costs (afc) gradually level off as output increases.

Figure 6.1 (c) shows average variable costs (avc) fall initially due to increasing returns, but rise as diminishing returns begin to operate. As more of the variable input, for example labour, is employed at a constant input price, disproportionately small increases in output lead to unit variable costs increasing.

Figure 6.1 (d) shows average total costs (atc) and reflects the impact of diminishing returns of the variable factor. The lowest point on the atc curve is defined as the optimum or best output level, that is the lowest unit cost.

Fig. 6.1 Costs - Behaviour

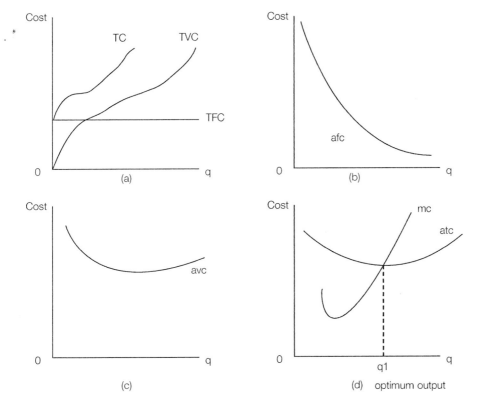

Marginal Cost, Marginal Revenue (MC, MR)

Marginal Cost (MC) is the extra or additional cost of producing one or more unit of output. It is the difference between successive total costs, i.e. MC11 = TC11 - TC10. So the MC of the 11th unit is equal to the total cost of 11, for example £100, less the total cost of 10, £93, or the marginal costs = £7. The marginal revenue is the extra revenue from selling one more unit of output. The MR of the 11th unit sold, is the total revenue of 11, for example £107, less the total revenue of 10, i.e. £100, so MR = £7. When MC = MR then it defines the most profitable or least loss output of the business so that TR - TC = maximum profit levels. The relationship between marginal and average total costs is shown in fig 6.1d

Costs/Revenue and the Output of the Firm

Table 6.1 Costs, Revenue and the Firm's Output (£'s)

Quantity	Labour @ 50p	Price	TVC	Total Revenue	Total Cost	Total Profit	Marginal Revenue	Marginal Cost	
0		20	0	0	14.5	-14.5	+0	+14.5	
1	6	18	3	18	17.5	+0.5	+18	+3.0	
2	11	16	5.5	32	20	+12	+14	+2.5	
3	15	14	7.5	42	22	+20	+10	+2.0	
(2) 4	21	12	10.5	48	25	+23	+6	+3)	MR = MC around 4 plus
5	31	10	15.5	50	30	+20	+2	+5)	
6	45	8	22.5	48	37	+11	-2	+7	
7	63	6	6.3	42	46	-4	-6	+9	
8	85	4	8.5	32	57	-5	-10	+11	

Table 6.1 illustrates total revenue (price x quantity sold), and total cost (fixed plus variable) and hence total profit, also MR, MC for a firm.

Notes

1. **Total Cost.** At zero output total costs is £14.5 so fixed costs must be £14.50 for all levels of output. Total variable costs is the difference between TC and TFC, i.e. £3.0, £5.5, £7.5, £10.5, £15.5, £22.5, £31.5, £42.5. If the cost of the variable labour input is £.5 each, then variable labour input increases (from zero to eight units of

output) as follows: 6, 11, 15, 21, 31, 45, 63, 85, i.e. proportionately less labour input to overall output, so diminishing returns applies.

2. The profit maximising output is approximately at 4 units of output. Here total cost is £25.0, total revenue is £48.0 and total profit is £23.0. From 0 to 4 output units the extra output increase provides extra slices of profit which increase overall profits, but beyond 4 units there are negative profit slices which decrease overall total profits.

3. Figure 6.2 based upon table 6.1 shows the behaviour of MC and MR intersecting at around 4 units of output. Between zero and four contributions to profit are positive, see area x, but after 4 units marginal cost exceeds marginal revenue so contributions are negative, see area y. (fig. 6.3). Revenue and profit behaviour as output changes and corresponds to the behaviour in figure 6.2 above.

4. Figure 6.4 shows the behaviour of average unit cost (AC) as well as marginal cost (MC). Initially marginal cost falls and then rises rapidly cutting AC at its lowest point. When MC is below AC, AC is falling, and when MC is above AC, AC is rising to MC cuts AC at its lowest point. An example from cricket illustrates. If a batsman has an average of 50 in 10 games, a total of 500 runs, and the marginal score is 40 then his average falls below 50 and vice versa if his marginal score is 60. In figure 6.4 with an output of 4 units average cost is £6.25, price is £12 so unit profit is £5.75 as shown by the arrow.

5. Applications of Price and Cost Changes, see figures 6.5, 6.6. If demand increases and price rises at all levels then MR shifts to the right, or left if price falls, and a new profit maximising output is determined as shown in figure 6.5. A price fall shifts MR to MR1 and optimum output reduces to 2 units whilst a price rise shifts MR to MR1 and optimum output reduces to 2 units whilst a price rise shifts MR to MR2 and output increases to 8 units. The impact of cost changes on output depend upon whether the cost change affects MC or AC, see figure 6.6. If variable costs rise, due to rising labour costs of VAT, the MC shifts upwards from MC to MC1 and optimum output reduces below 4 units. If fixed costs rise overall, perhaps due to a rise in a lump sum tax or if fixed costs rise, then MC is unchanged but AC increased, i.e. from AC to AC1. This means output remains at 4 units, but unit and overall profit levels fall.

Long Run Costs and the Envelope Curve

As the plant and equipment is added the scale of production increase and the firm moves, see figure 6.7, from short run average cost (SRAC1) to SRAC 2, etc., with the short run marginal cost (SRMC) cutting SRAC at its lowest point. In the long run plant size is variable and so eventually long-run costs increase as short-run costs increase exhibiting diminishing returns. By joining up the lowest cost points on the SRAC curves as shown in figure 6.8 we can obtain an envelope curve of these points which describe the minimum attainable long- run average costs (LRAC). The long run marginal cost (LRMC) is constructed on the same basis and it will cut the LRAC curve at its lowest point. Point B is where LRAC is minimised

Fig. 6.2

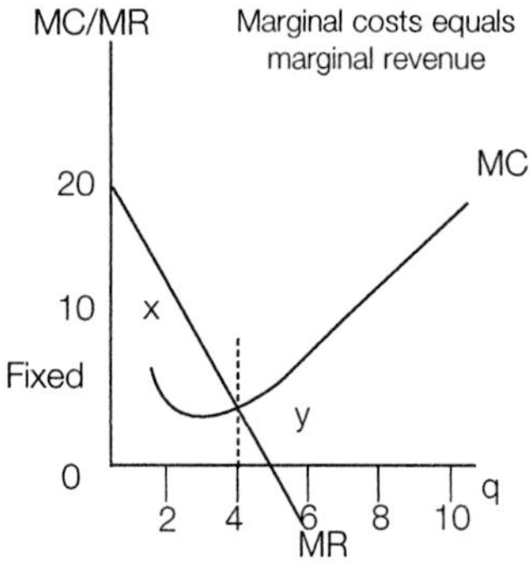

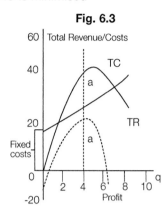

Fig. 6.3

Fig. 6.4

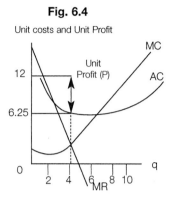

Fig. 6.5

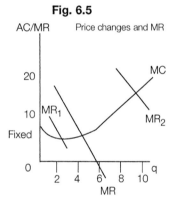

Fig. 6.6

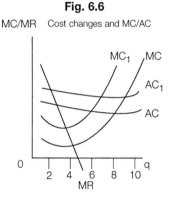

and shows the long run optimum or capacity in the industry. The downward part of the of the LRAC is explained by economies of scale and represents decreasing costs whilst the upward part of the LRAC is due to diseconomies of scale representing increasing costs. In the real world manufacturing businesses often experience constant returns and costs as figure 6.8 shows. The output level where costs are minimised is defined as the minimum scale of efficiency (the MSE) and this depends upon each individual industry.

Also the slope for the LRAC can be gradual or steep, as figure 6.8 shows

Fig. 6.7 Long-Run Cost Behaviour = Envelope Curve of Short-Run Costs in an Industry

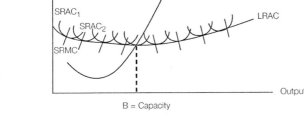

B = Capacity

Fig. 6.8 Long-Run Manufacturing Cost Behaviour

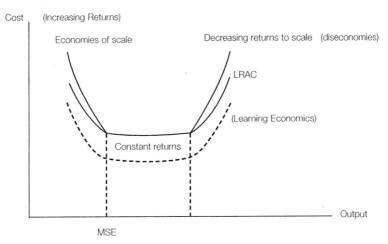

MSE

Economies of Scale (Internal)

These operate to reduce long-run unit costs and are under control of the firm. They are experienced by manufacturing industries and are as follows (in note form):

Production or Technical Economies

Large firms are able to increase the scope for division of labour and specialisation which enables them to use more capital intensive machinery and specialised equipment. By building larger capital units the economies of increased dimensions can be further exploited. In the manufacturing industry robotic techniques of production and automated and computerised technologies are examples of these technical economies.

Financial Economies

The large firm is able to tap larger sources of finance which enables it to borrow at lower interest rates and experience better credit facilities. Furthermore, it is able to sell shares and obtain capital at relatively cheap rates.

Risk-Bearing Economies

This is for a large conglomerate - the ability to spread risk across a variety of product markets.

Marketing Economies

These are experienced by large firms on both the buying and selling side of the business. They are such things as discounts due to buying in bulk, national advertising and brand names, the ability to control input quality, specialised buying staff, and preferential transport and sales rates.

Managerial and Administrative Economies

These cover such items as specialised boards of directors, one unified accounting department using centralised computerised systems and also specialised professional managers.

Learning Economies

If a management team can improve its efficiency by learning as more of the same operations are undertaken, then over a period of time, and as technology improves, learning efficiencies will influence the whole business and hence overall costs will fall as is shown in figure 6.8.

Economies of Scope

This is when there is a specialised knowledge of such things as machinery or technology which can be shared across different products, for example British Aerospace produce aircraft and cars.

Diseconomies of Scale (Internal)

The increase in scale often brings problems and therefore costs can rise as firms grow beyond their optimum size. These diseconomies derive from labour usage and associated problems of man-management. Therefore communications coordination and control become difficult as departments increase in scale and size. This leads to workers becoming less involved in the business decision-making process and labour disputes, such as strikes, can increase and lead to cost rises.

Economies of Scale (External)

External economies of scale result from the growth of an industry in a particular region or area. These economies increase the efficiency of the business and hence lower units costs. They are locational and can take a variety of forms, such as :

- a skilled labour force with training facilities;
- the nearness of component suppliers and sub-contract workers;
- a good communications and information systems close at hand;
- a developed infrastructure with road and rail links;
- associated and complementary product markets in the vicinity.

These external economies explain why financial institutions locate in the City of London.

The Business Decision : Output Levels in the Short and Long Run

In both the long and short run the best output level for the firm will be where marginal cost equals marginal revenue. At this output level the decision is then whether to produce or not. In the short run the firm will produce so long as price or average revenue equals or exceeds average variable costs because in the short run fixed costs have to be paid and so can be disregarded, that is bygones are bygones. However, in the long run the firm will only produce so long as price covers average total costs, and it makes the least normal profits. If average costs are not covered, the firm will go out of business in the long run as figure 6.9 illustrates. In the short run , so long as price is op or more production at Oq will be viable because op covers average variable costs. A price above Op, in the price region 'a', will provide a positive contribution to fixed costs and above a price region 'a', will produce a positive contribution to fixed costs and above a price of p1 abnormal profits are earned. In the long run at output oq price must be at least Op1, or the firm will go out of business. This means that at any price above Op1, in price region b, abnormal profit will be made by the firm.

Fig. 6.9 Production in the Short and Long Run

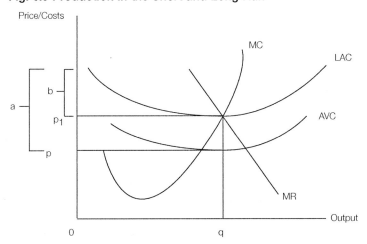

Market Structures

The optimum output of the firm will be determined by equating marginal cost to marginal revenue. Abnormal profit is calculated as the difference between price (average revenue) and average unit cost. Since markets differ the behaviour of the firm will change depending upon market structures. It is important to note that business behaviour will vary because firms operate in different market types at different times, for example a competitive firm may become a monopolist and vice versa. The behaviour of the firms under each market structure is outlined.

Table 6.2 Classification of Market Structures

Characteristics	(i) Competitive	(ii) Monopolistic Competition	(iii) Oligopolistic	(iv) Monopolistic
1. MSE (output)	Small	Variable	Intermediate	Large
2. Business units in industry	Many	Many	Few	One
3. Price determination	Supply & Demand	Monopolistic Potential Entrants	Oligopolist or Cartel	Monopolistic or Overseas pressure
4. Entry barriers	None	None	Agreements brand proliferation	Low Cost or barriers
5. Example (industry)	Chicago grain market	Corner shop Computer software	Petrol Retailing Brewers High Street Grocers Taxi Rank	British Telecom NHS/NCB Water Boards

Table 6.2 shows different market structures. Each will be analysed, starting with competitive markets.

Perfectly Competitive Market Conditions

The Chicago Grain Market

Perfectly competitive markets are a highly idealised type and rarely exist in the real world. The conditions which create such a market are :

- Freedom of entry and exit to the market for the buyer and seller. This means there is costless entry and exit (see Contestable Markets) and this implies perfect mobility of goods and factors of production.

- Similarity or homogeneity of products, where all goods, services and factors of production bought and sold are identical.

- Perfect knowledge, where everyone has full information regarding market price.

■ It is possible to buy and sell any amount of the product or factor at the going market price.

■ There is no government interference which distorts market conditions, such as taxation.

■ There is a large number of competitive buyers and sellers acting independently so no one firm or group of firms is able to influence market price.

If these conditions are relaxed, it is possible for imperfectly competitive market structures, such as monopolies, to develop in both product and factor markets.

Competitive Markets and the Firm's Revenue

In view of the above conditions, overall market forces of supply and demand set the price in the competitive product market. If the product is identical, for example cucumbers, the consumer will only pay the market price and so the producer becomes a price taker in the sense that the demand for his cucumbers can be viewed as perfectly elastic at the going market price. This means the producer cannot influence the market price. If any attempt is made by the producer to sell cucumbers above the going price, consumers will not buy but will see out cheaper market prices for cucumbers. Figure 6.10 illustrates the market price for cucumbers is 10p each, see (i), and this means the producer can sell as many as he likes at 10p. Thus total revenue increases as follows: 10p, 20p, 30p, 40p etc., for each additional cucumber sold. The extra revenue or marginal revenue is always 10p and so the average revenue is also 10p, i.e. the same as the price. This is shown as a horizontal line for the producer at 10p or 15p, in the event that demand pushes up market price in 6.10 (ii). The total revenue (TR) for the producer at 10p and 15p, is shown in (iii) and here TR increases at a constant rate for both 10p and 15p market prices.

Fig. 6.10 Changing Market Price and its impact upon the revenue of the firm

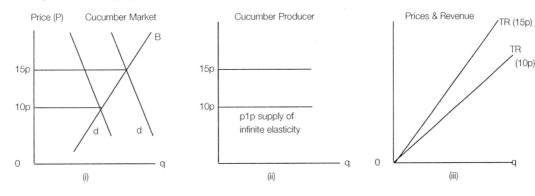

The Equilibrium of the Firm and the Industry in the Short Run

In the short run the firm will experience diminishing returns so both marginal and average cost will increase and be U shaped. The firm will continue in business in the short run so long as it covers its average variable costs; though it will hope to cover all its costs and even make above normal profits. Figure 6.11 (a) and (b) illustrate short-run equilibrium for the industry and the firm. Initially, industry cucumber prices are 10p and at this level mc = mr at oq output for the firm. At this price, average variable costs are just covered so any price below 10p will lead to the firm immediately going out of business because ongoing variable expenses such as wages cannot be paid. In other words, at 10p a cucumber the producer is a loss maker. If demand pushes up prices to 12p per cucumber, the producer is now able to cover all costs; p = atc so normal profits are earned in this case by the marginal firm and as price increases again to 15p supernormal profits are earned at Op1, where mc = mr2, since price is now above average total cost. The extra output produced by the producer/s i.e. Oq1, Oq2 is identified by the arrow in figure 6.11 (a) and for the industry is shown by the slope of the combined individual producers supply when this is above average variable costs.

Fig. 6.11

Short-term market demand changes

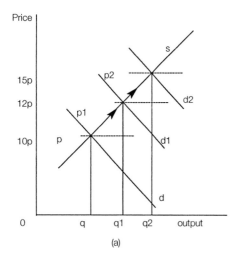

(a)

The behaviour of the firm in the short term

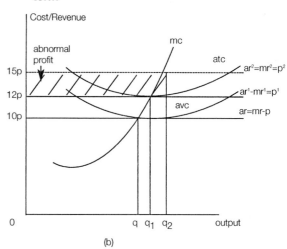

(b)

The Equilibrium of the Firm in the Long Run

In the long run the firm is able to view all factors of production as variable and will seek the lowest cost limits of factor input. Furthermore, free entry into the industry means firms will be able to come and go without incurring costs. The firm will now be on its long-run average and marginal cost schedules. The behaviour of the industry and firm in adjusting to long- run equilibrium is shown in figure 6.12. Initially the market price is 10p a cucumber which is in the long run equilibrium in the market for the industry so oq is the capacity or optimum output. In this case, assume all firms have similar costs, so the LRATC for each firm is identical. By definition, for any given LRATC there will also be a short-run average total costs (SRATC) and marginal cost which in this case will be the same as the long-run equivalent, (LRMC=SRMC). If demand now increases to d2 at a price of 15p, short-run output increases to Oq1 where firms now make abnormal profits because price exceeds short-run and long-run average costs. In the long run, the output of the existing suppliers increases and new entrants are attracted into the industry which shifts supply to s1. There are now more producers in the industry and this pushes price down to 10p, s to s1, and wipes out abnormal profits for the industry. Also, industry output at Oq2 is stable in the long run and Oq is the long-run optimum output for each firm - assuming each firm's costs are identical.

Fig. 6.12 Long run equilibrium for Industry and Competitive Firm

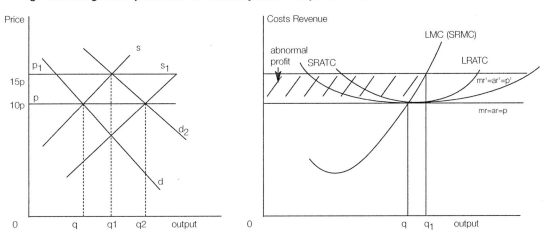

In the real world this is unlikely because some firms will have invested in newer plant than others, so in the long run some may still be making abnormal profits whilst others will be making losses. Furthermore, in the long run each firm's output will be more flexible (elastic), above total average costs and this is shown for both firm and industry in LMRC and LRS in figure 6.13 (a) and (b).

Fig. 6.13 The Firm

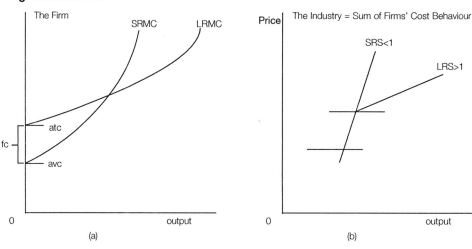

Supply Price in the Long Run

In the very long run demand changes, shown in figure 6.14 by d to d2, will, after firms enter and leave the industry, influence long run price depending upon cost and supply conditions. Figure 6.14 a,b,c, show industry cost behaviour varying from constant, decreasing or increasing factor input costs. Note that in the short run input costs are constant but in the long run diminishing or increasing returns can lead to factor costs changing. The stable price of op1 (LRS1 in figure 6.14 (a)) reflects constant supply costs as new firms enter or leave the industry. This is because they use such small amounts of total factor inputs that they have no effect on overall input costs. In figure 6.14(b) LRS2, costs decrease because the extra output allows suppliers of factor inputs to increase specialisation and reduce factor input costs over the whole industry; the industry experiences external economies of scale. Finally, in figure 6.14 (c) LRS3, expansion by new and existing firms bids up the long-run price of factor inputs so marginal costs rise and long-run supply shifts upwards. Thus overall demand changes can affect market price in the long run. With a decreasing cost industry (LRS2) a fall in demand will lead to rise in factor costs and product costs, but when demand increases factor costs and long-run prices fall.

Fig. 6.14 The Behaviour of Long Run Industry Price and Supply

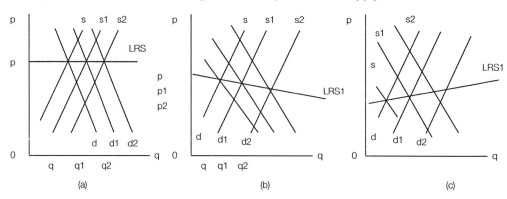

Data Response 1

Transport Costs Compared

The diagram shows the hypothetical relationship between transportation and the volume of goods carried.

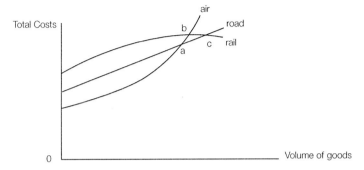

1. Comment upon the fixed and variable cost components for the three modes of transport.
2. Compare the behaviour of marginal costs in each case.
3. What do the points a, b and c indicate?
4. Identify which transport mode you would use in the case of diamonds, tomatoes and coal and give a brief economic explanation.

Data Response 2

Full Cost or Marginal Cost Pricing

		Products	
Cost Per Unit £	A	B	C
Materials	2.8	5.2	3.4
Labour	3.6	4.0	5.1
Overheads (200% of labour)	7.2	8.0	10.2
Total Cost	13.6	17.2	18.7
Price	15.7	16.1	20.2
Annual Sales	15,000	20,000	18,000

The accountant provides the above information and advises that Product B should be discontinued as it makes a loss of £1.1/unit x 20,000, i.e. £22,000 p.a

Further inspection shows that 40% of overheads are fixed. Should Product B be maintained or discontinued? Give reasons for your answer.

Data Response 3

Cost Behaviour

The diagram below shows the short-run average total cost functions of three hypothetical companies, A, B and C.

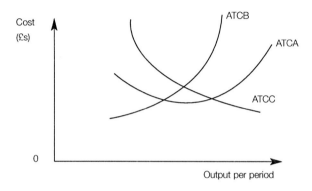

1. What would you expect to be the characteristics of firms A and C?
2. Which, of firms A and B, is the most efficient, and why?

Data Response 4

Successive Units of Output	Total Cost (£)	Average Cost (£)	Marginal Cost (£)
1	20	20	20
2	32		
3		14	
4			6
5	50		

Use the data in the above table to calculate:
   a. total cost at an output of 4 units
   b. average cost when marginal cost is £12
   c. marginal cost when average cost is £10.

Data Response 5

Study the following data which gives details of development and production costs in the United Kingdom motor car manufacturing industry.

Output of cars (thousand cars p.a. for 4 years)	100	250	500	1000	2000
Initial costs for model (£ million)	40	50	60	80	110
Costs per car produced over 4 year run:					
Initial costs, £	100	50	30	20	14
Materials and bought-in components £	290	270	255	247	240
Labour (direct and indirect) £	120	100	92	87	84
Capital charges for fixed and working capital £	75	65	58	53	48
Total ex-works cost £	585	485	435	407	386

(Source: C F Pratten, *Economics of Scale in Manufacturing Industry,* Cambridge University Press)

Notes:
1. The initial costs include the cost of designing a new model, building prototypes and 'tooling up' i.e. investing in extra fixed capital equipment.
2. The output assumes a new model is produced for a period of four years.

a. What does the data indicate about the effect of increases in car output on (i) initial costs and (ii) costs other than initial costs?

b. Explain you answer to part (a).

c. What policy implications for motor car manufacturers are suggested by the data?

Data Response 6

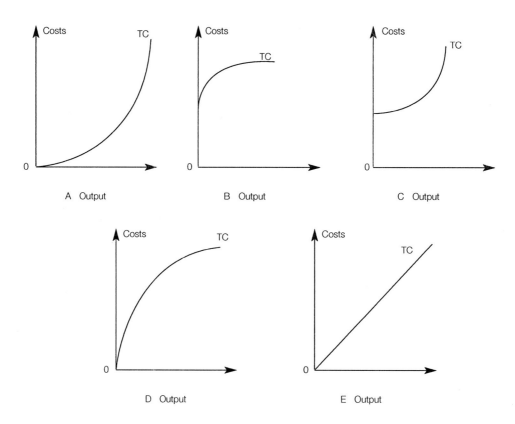

A firm has no fixed costs and experiences decreasing returns to scale.

Which diagram (A-E above) represents the firm's total cost curve?

Data Response 7

Study the data below which relate to a British Airways scheduled flight between London and New York.

The economics of a scheduled Boeing 747-400 flight from London to New York

Revenues

First class: 18 seats   Ticket price £2000

Business class: 74 seats   Ticket price £1100

Economy class: 294 seats   Ticket price £350

Note: Economy class may be subject to a variety of conditions, for example, a minimum stay period of six nights including a Saturday and/or 21 days advance booking.

Costings

Flight crew, salaries and expenses to include captain, first officer, engineer, chief steward, three pursers and 13 stewards	£ 9,250
Aircraft fuel and oil	£11,882
Landing fees and navigation charges	£ 9,920
Passenger services to include catering (two meals for the eight-hour flight), free gifts of comfort packs and drinks	£15,870
Ground services to include aircraft maintenance for the flight, aircraft cleaning, baggage handling, check-in and other airport facilities	£17,200
Contribution to airline overheads, including general administration, advertising and promotion, depreciation, ticket sales, aircraft overhauls, insurance.	£68,350

(Source Lloyds Link)

1. Using the data given answer the following questions.

   a. If the airline had sold all its first class and business seats, how many economy class seats would it have to sell in order to cover costs?

   b. Calculate the airline's profit per flight if it sold all seats.

2. What are the conditions necessary for price discrimination?
   With reference to the data, how far do these apply in the case of an airline?

3. Using examples from the data, distinguish between the fixed and variable costs of transatlantic flight.

Data Response 8

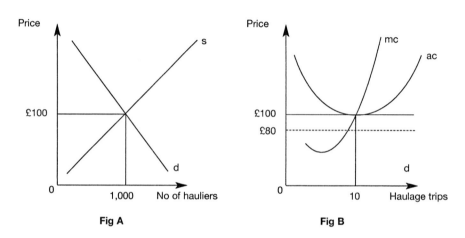

Fig A

Fig B

The UK road haulage business is a competitive market with industry and firm conditions shown in fig A and B respectively. It is suggested lower diesel tax would reduce the average cost to £80 - see Fig B, and make the industry more profitable.

1. Use Fig B and show what happens when diesel price falls in the short term.

2. What will be the medium term impact of this policy on the industry?

3. What will be the long term impact on the hauliers profits?

4. In the absence of the above diesel tax policy how else could hauliers earn super normal profits?

chapter seven

The Economic Behaviour of the Monopolist/Oligopolist and Monopolistic Competition

Aims

To define, explain and discuss

- The Behaviour of the Monopolist in the Short and Long Run
- Monopolistic Competition
- Short and Long Run Equilibrium and Barriers to Entry
- Monopolists and Price Discrimination
- The Nature of Oligopolistic Markets
- Collusive and Competitive Models of Behaviour
- Strategic Entry Deterrence and Game Theory
- The Competitive Fringe and the Dominant Firm

Key Concepts

Barriers to Entry; Price Greater than MC; Abnormal Profits; Competition, Price Discrimination; Interdependence v Independence; Cost Plus; Price Stability; Kinked Demand Curve; Game Theory; Strategic Entry Barriers; Competitive Fringe

Definition

Monopoly in the product or factor market indicates the existence of a sole supplier or buyer (monopsonist). The monopoly can take the form of a dominant firm, or a group of producers who act as if they were a monopoly (a cartel). Monopolies arise for a variety of reasons, such as cost barriers to entry, etc. Instead of being a price taker they face their own demand schedule and are able to set a price or an output level but not both unless demand is completely inelastic. The demand conditions given in the table 7.1. The price, quantity demanded schedule, is the same as the average revenue for the monopolist and the marginal revenue curve slopes downwards at twice the rate of average revenue.

Table 7.1

Price (p)	Quantity (q)	T.R.	M.R.	AR=Demand
10	2	20		10
9	3	27 >	7	9
8	4	32 >	5	8
7	5	35>	3	7
6	6	36>	1	6

The Equilibrium of the Monopolist in the Short/Long Run

Figure 7.1 shows average and marginal revenue behaviour together with marginal and average costs which reflect diminishing returns for the monopolist. This can now be used to analyse the short- and long-run behaviour of the monopolist. In the short and long run the profit maximising monopolist will set output where marginal cost equates with marginal revenue, and at this output (3) price will set to demand or average revenue, i.e. £8. In the short run, with barriers to entry, the monopolist has no competition and makes abnormal profits as shown in figure 7.2 (i) If barriers exist in the long run, these profits will continue to be made. However, in the long run it is likely that new firms will enter the market and reduce these barriers and/or governments will reduce these market constraints, for example by outlawing restrictive practices, which both reduce demand and marginal revenue so that only normal profits are earned, as shown in figure 7.2(ii).

Fig. 7.1 Monopolist Behaviour of mr, ar

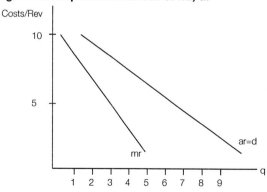

Table 7.2 Short and Long Run with Barriers to Entry

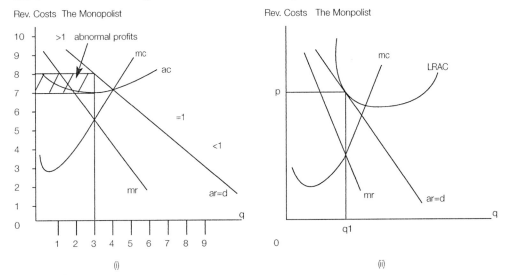

Demand Elasticity and the Monopolist

As discussed demand schedule, similar to the one facing the monopolist, varies from an elasticity of more than 1(>1) at the top of the curve, to an elasticity of less than 1 (<1) for lower prices at the bottom of the demand curve.   This means that the monopolist will price somewhere between the elastic range at the top (high prices) to the mind-point where price elasticity is equal to 1 (unity). If the monopolist reduces the price into the inelastic region at the bottom of the demand schedule, total revenue and profits will fall. Only monopolies with other than profit maximising objectives will be able to reduce price into this region in order to maximise market share or other sales objectives.

Barriers to Entry

Monopolies in the form of a dominant firm or cartel are able to exclude potential competitors by a variety of barriers. These are as follows.

Cost Advantages

Economies of scale and other efficiencies enable costs to reduce to such a low level, especially for natural monopolies, that competition is excluded. These natural cost barriers exist in the distribution of gas, electricity, and telecommunications services, etc. (See sections on Limit Entry Pricing and Natural Monopolies below).

Patents, Licences and Copyright

A patent protects a firm from competition and is important to high-tech industries, such as Rank Xerox who by virtue of patent rights had the whole UK market for dry copying in the 1960s and made large profits. Copyright given to authors is a protection of intellectual property and stops copying in the book publishing market. A licence to provide a service is often required before a business is able to supply, for example taxi cabs and independent regional television companies. Cable and satellite TV is now providing competition for regional independent television monopolists.

Capital Needs

Certain industries, such as manufacturing, require huge capital investment before production can take place, for example chemicals. Not only will the amount of the investment deter potential entrants but the likelihood of failure and the associated costly exit from the industry means business units will hesitate before entering this type of industry.

Product Advertising

Consumer goods industries are dominated by monopolists who have, over the years, spent heavily on brand advertising in order to differentiate their produce in the eyes of the consumer and so earn consumer loyalty, for example Coca-Cola and Kellogg's Cornflakes. A would-be competitor needs to overcome this advantage which may require substantial advertising investment. At the same time, national advertising leads to economies of scale in marketing, so when demand increases the firm is able to increase its minimum scale of efficiency and hence entry cost barriers become larger.

Channels of Distribution/Locational Advantages

Existing firms in the market may have a high degree of control over the channels of distribution which means new entrants are unable to sell their products on a large scale. One alleged restrictive practice is retail maintenance on books and records. Sales product prices are fixed and producers can exclude new entrants wishing to reduce price by blacklisting retail outlets if they do not maintain these controlled prices. A similar barrier in the retail sector is when a retail outlet has a locational monopoly position which gives it a special advantage over its competitors.

Strategic Entry Barriers

These barriers are deliberately set up by incumbent firms in order to deter would-be new entrants. They take a variety of forms ranging from: heavy advertising expenditure on the existing range of products; developing a product mix so that there are no market niches or openings for a new brand; the development of capacity which enables the encumbent to cut costs and prices. These strategies are designed to put off competitors and work so long as the threats of the incumbent firm are credible and believable.

Government-Created Barriers

Acts of Parliament create privileged state monopolies. These range from the granting of licences to supply a television service, for example the BBC, the creation of nationalised industries to supply a service for example British Rail, or the provision of education of health care, for example the NHS.

Barriers to market entry ensure that supernormal profits are earned and, the greater these profits, the greater the incentive for competitors to enter a market. Schumpeter argued that monopoly powers cannot last for ever as profits act as a spur to new entrants and existing monopolies try to reduce the threat of competition by continually inventing new products in order to maintain their profit levels. Schumpeter defined this as a process of 'creative destruction' whereby existing firms try to create new products whilst new firms try to destroy the control of existing firms by inventing better and more suitable products.

Limit Pricing Barriers

If the monopolist maximises short-run profit where mc = mr, i.e. at 3 units, there is room for a new entrant because average costs (AC) are lower than £8 (see figure 7.2(i)). If costs initially are below entry price, then new entrants could come into the market unless the existing supplier artificially keeps price below costs and increases output to prevent entry in the long run. Then the new entrant will find the price always below start-up average costs and so limit pricing excludes new competition. This practice is sometimes referred to as predatory pricing. In this case (see figure 7.2) the firm will attempt to prevent new entrants by pricing at £7 and producing up to 5 units, ((the competitive equilibrium). This means average costs at £8, for new entrants, will be higher than a price at £7 in the short run so losses will be incurred. The monopolist will, in the long run, without any competition, increase price to £8 and make abnormal profits because would-be entrants have now been forced out of the market.

Monopolistic Competition

Monpolistic competition is where there are many different, often small, firms producing goods and services which are differentiated from each other in at least one respect. They are close but not perfect substitutes. Since the products are sufficiently alike, new entrants may come into the market and produce a slightly different product which will reduce demand for the output of the existing firms. The ease of entry into the market is the essential condition so, in the case of school and college book publishing, copyright on the author and title provides a monopoly right to the publisher. However, new firms can easily enter the market and produce a similar book which reduces sales of the existing title.

Diagrammatically the short-and long-term situation of the profit-maximising monpolistically competitive firm can be seen in figure 7.3. The firm faces the downward -sloping demand curve of the monopolist AR1 and marginal revenue Mr1, with its average and marginal cost AC, MC. At output OX1 the firm will be maximising profit and pricing at Op1 and making supernormal profits. In the long run as new firms enter the market, the demand of the existing firm will reduce and will move inwards on the diagram until supernormal profits are reduced to zero. Here the demand curve AR2 is at a tangent to AC and normal profits only are earned at output OX2. Furthermore, as output reduces from OX1 to OX2 there will be surplus capacity within the firm and an increase in output (from OX2) would lower unit costs and thus increase cost efficiency.

Fig. 7.3 Monopolistic Competition

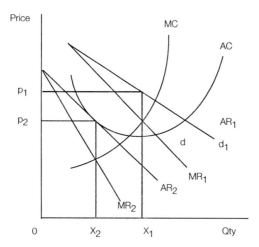

In the above analysis it was assumed that the firm tried to maximise profits where marginal costs equal marginal revenue. In the real world this may not be the case. Businessmen do not always understand that profit maximising implies mc = mr and even if they did they may not be able to provide sufficiently accurate costs and revenue information show in how each changed with respect to the extra unit produced or sold. Assuming they could provide this amount of detail the administration necessary may prove too costly in terms of extra accounting, staff, etc. Furthermore, they may be deterred from pricing where profits are maximised since they may fear competition from new entrants which could ultimately reduce their profits. If the firm announced that a particular range of school and college titles sold were very profitable, new entrants could come into the market and eventually only normal profit would be earned. Indeed, union wage negotiators who saw high profits would immediately increase their demands and bid up wage costs in the industry, which the firm may not be able to match, especially if it had a poor cash flow. Excessive profits could antagonise customers and lead to government action in the form of a monopolies commission investigation, etc.

Furthermore, both businessmen's behaviour and newer economic theories suggest that profit maximising is not the sole nor the most important objective of the firm. The firm could set price to maximise its market share or its sales revenue. Most firms in these markets offer a range of products so their long-term relationship with both retailers, wholesales and customers have to be considered. These may be best suited to a less-than-profit maximising price. 'Satisficing' theories, associated with Simon, Cyert and March, suggest firms set prices which provide a satisfactory level of profits, wages, taxation, etc. Indeed where the firm is a government-run nationalised industry, it may be attempting to offer a national level of service which may lead to a break-even only price level. Indeed, Professors Machlup and Stigler argue that even if businessmen do not know about marginal costs and marginal revenue they still act "as if" their long-term objective is to maximise profit by equalising overall predicted changes in revenue and cost.

Monopolies and Third Degree Price Discrimination

Price discrimination occurs when different buyers or groups of buyers are charged different prices for the same good/s - assuming the costs of production are the same for the producer. The economic reason for this practice is that profits are higher (or losses are less) than if a uniform price were charged to all buyers.

Economic theory predicts two necessary conditions for successful price discrimination. Firstly the elasticity of demand must differ between buyers and secondly it must be physically possible to segment the market and prevent leakages taking place between consumers being charged different prices. If it is not possible to separate markets then arbitrage takes place and the consumer charged the low price sells the product to the buyer charged the high price until an equilibrium prevails with a uniform rate throughout both markets; discrimination is only economic if the cost of separating markets is less than the extra revenue generated.

These two conditions can only apply when a single seller, the monopolistic, exists in the market and the economic case for price discrimination can be shown graphically in figure 7.4.

Fig. 7.4 Monopolies and Price Discrimination

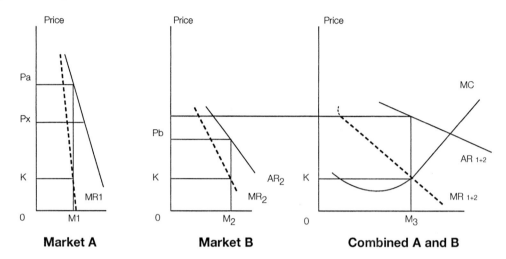

| Market A | Market B | Combined A and B |

Figure 7.4 shows the monopolist selling into two distinct markets, A and B. In the absence of price discrimination marginal cost and revenue conditions would indicate a uniform price of Px in both markets. The price would be too low in market A and too high in market B. If the markets could be separated the intersection of the combined MR/MC would now indicate separate output/prices in both markets of Pa and Pb (where individual MR/MC intersections occur) at K. This exploits the consumers' inelastic demand in market A, giving more profit and revenue, and in market B the gain in demand increases revenue as the price falls because of the elastic nature of demand (see prices Pa, Pb).

Price discrimination occurs in a host of markets though its economic basis varies. Geographical price discrimination occurs when regions or countries pay different prices for the same product. Thus UK car buyers pay more for a Mini Metro than purchasers of the same car in Belgium, France, Germany etc. This helps Rover make more profit on the UK market though cost conditions are roughly similar in both market areas. This geographical variation in price occurs in other sectors. The American air traveller pays far less per mile for internal USA flights, because of cut price competition, than for transatlantic air travel where scheduled flights are priced high to exploit the UK businessman's inelastic demand.

In book publishing it is common practice for UK publishers to sell the exclusive geographical distribution rights to another distributor or publisher. The same book can bear two prices on its back cover, a UK price and, say, an Australian price, and the UK publisher is unable to sell into the Australian market. Even after handling charges have been deducted the Australian price represents a very high sterling price equivalent and very often Australian purchasers try to buy direct from the UK publisher at the lower UK price. Whilst the UK publisher may refuse to sell to Australia, in view of the exclusive sales agreement, leakage may still occur if other UK booksellers sell directly into the Australian market. Therefore, even though price discrimination agreements exist if the price differential is high enough, attempts at 'buying round', that is purchasing directly at the lower UK, price will be difficult to stop completely.

Price discrimination often occurs on the basis of time. Off-peak telephone calls are lowest late at night, early in the morning or at weekends. Commuters on British Rail pay higher charges for peak travel than tourists or shoppers going into London during late morning or early afternoon.

The status of the buyer is again an important consideration. The unemployed and elderly receive low-priced benefits on the railway, at the cinema or at football matches, etc. Children are often charged lower prices for travel and holidays, even though they consume the same amounts as adults.

Theoretically the aggregate demand schedule incorporates a number of individual demand preferences and therefore reflects different elasticities of demand. If this is the case, the logical outcome of a price discrimination policy is to charge an almost infinite number of prices to different individuals along the demand schedule which would help the firm maximise its profits or, in the case of British Rail, reduce its loss. However, separating the market into this number of segments proves almost impossible in practice and explains why it is only done in most markets in a piecemeal manner.

Price Discrimination - First /Second Degree

First degree price discrimination is when the firm can sell each unit at the maximum price that each individual customer is willing to pay. See Fig 7.5 (a). The first unit is sold for £10, the second for £9, the third for £8 and so on. The demand curve becomes its marginal revenue as price equals revenue gained from each extra unit. Profit maximisation occurs at 4 units where mr=mc. The triangle above £7 represents total revenue and profits and shows the loss of consumers surplus. Second degree price discrimination is when for example an airline sells off any excess capacity seating at a lower than standard price. Aircrafts have high fixed costs but low marginal costs eg catering costs. The marginal costs of seats are constant until capacity is reached when mc rises vertically at eg 300 seats as in fig 7.5 (b). The profit maximising optimum is for 100 seats selling for £300. The excess capacity of 200 seats ie 300 less 100, can be sold off, on a standby basisat the cheaper price of £200. This process could also mean seat prices between £300 and £200. This would maximise the yield from the plane and also shows why hotels charge different prices for the same room.

Fig. 7.5 a First Degree Price Discrimination

Fig. 7.5 b Second Degree Price Discrimination

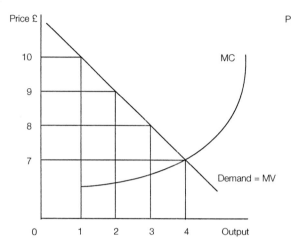

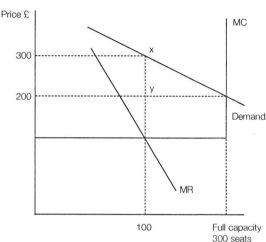

Oligopolistic Markets

Oligopolistic markets are those dominated by a few firms, usually similar in size, who behave in either a competitive or non-competitive (collusive) manner. There are so few sellers that each firm is affected by the action of its rivals; unlike monopolies whose barriers to entry protect the market from competition. Thus the behaviour of the oligopolist is interdependant; it depends upon the action of its rivals whilst monopolies behave independently of each other. Oligopolistic structures are commonplace in markets such as steel production, petrol retailing and high street banking where products and services are very similar. Oligopolists also operate where brand differentiation is high, for example the market for cars, beer and bread.

Characteristics of Oligopolistic Markets

Oligopolistic markets are, by definition, heavily concentrated so much of an industry's output is in the hands of a few producers, for example the CR5 = 70% etc., which means the five largest producers are likely to have over 70% of the market output. Research has shown also that in the UK and the USA:

- Oligopolistic industrial concentration ratios are increasing in manufacturing sectors.
- Profit rates are usually higher in the more concentrated market sectors.

- Product advertising and non-price competition is commonplace.

- Average variable and marginal costs are saucer-shaped under oligopoly, i.e. they often appear 'L' shaped.

- Unlike perfectly competitive and monopolistic market models which predict a unique price/output combination, oligopoly behaviour suggests there is more than one output level where profit is maximised.

- Oligopolists often use a full variable cost plus profit mark-up formula in order to set price which then tends to be rather sticky compared to the volatile price movements in many competitive markets. This price stability is illustrated in figure 7.6 which shows the oligopolistic price charged at the pump by Shell compared to the free and volatile market price for petrol determined on the Rotterdam spot market during August/September 1990.

- Oligopolists compete or collude in markets. Table 7.2 outlines the circumstances under which each is likely to occur.

Fig. 7.6 Increases in Shell UK Pump Prices versus Increases in Rotterdam Spot Price (August - September 1990)

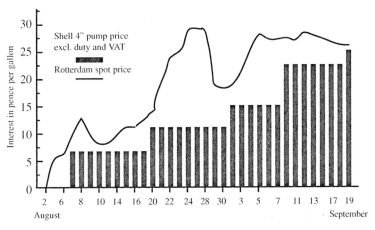

Source: Shell Shareholders Bulletin, Sept. 1990

Table 7.2 Oligopolies: Collusion or Competition

Factor	Encourages collusion:	Competition if:
Barriers to entry	✔	
Product is non-standard		✔
Demand and costs are stable	✔	
Collusion is legal	✔	
Secrecy about price and output		✔
Collusion is illegal		
Easy communication of price and output	✔	✔
Standard produce	✔	

Models of Oligopolistic Behaviour (Competitive)

A. The Monopolistic Model

Applying the above characteristics of oligopolistic markets, one explanatory model is illustrated in figure 7.7 which incorporates saucer-shaped costs together with a monopolistic theory of behaviour with respect to the change in demand from d2 to d1. This shows that, even with this change because of relatively flat average variable costs, the equating of marginal cost and marginal revenue means that the price is relatively stable at op1 between the output range oq and oq1. This also can be interpreted as a full variable cost plus fixed cost mark up as the figure illustrates. At the same time if similar sized oligopolies in an industry have similar costs and products, then it is not surprising to find similar and stable prices in these markets, for example in petrol retailing.

Fig. 7.7. A: Competitive Oligopolistic Behaviour

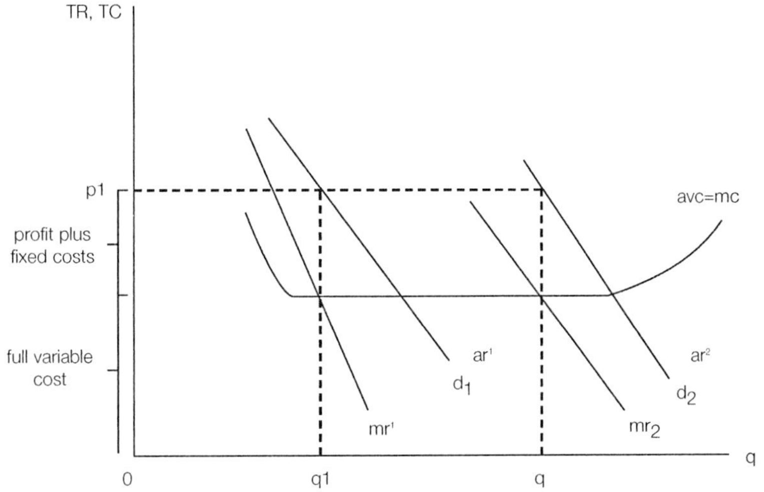

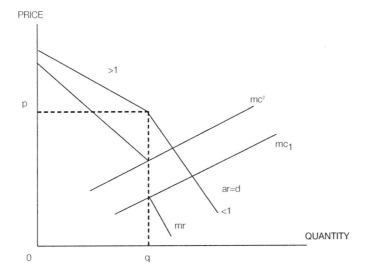

B. The Kinked Demand Theory

This theory assumes the demand facing the individual oligopolist is kinked at the current price level. The price stability at op, the kink, is determined because the firm believes that if it cuts this price its rivals will follow so no extra revenue is generated; demand is inelastic. Furthermore, if it raises its price its rivals will not follow suit so its revenue will suffer; demand is elastic. This is illustrated in figure 7.8 which shows the demand schedule and a discontinuous marginal revenue schedule. Thus even with a change in marginal cost from mc1 to mc2 the price stays at Op. However, this theory does not explain why the price is originally at Op.

Fig. 7.8 B: The Kinked Demand Curve

Fig. 7.9 C: Collusive Oligopolies

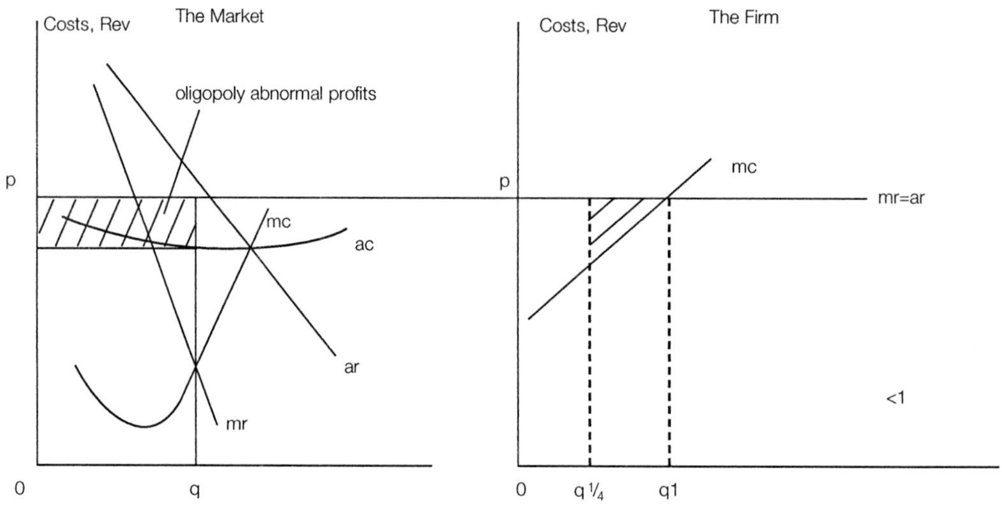

q $\frac{1}{4}$ = ogliopolists quota q1 = desired actual output

C. Collusive Oligopoly Models

The collusive cartel model is useful when there are a small number of firms selling a similar product and when a fierce price war would be harmful. In this case the firms recognise that a policy of mutual interdependence may help to maximise overall industry profit. If it is assumed they have similar costs they can be treated as if they were a single multiplant monpolist (see figure 7.9) This shows overall oligopolistic profits are maximised at a price/output level of Op/Oq. This output is then shared out between the oligopolists, for example a quarter or a fifth of the market to each one. However, even when marginal costs are the same for each firm, there will be a temptation for each to break ranks and supply more than the allocated share, i.e. Oq$\frac{1}{4}$, because the ruling prices appear as a constant marginal revenue to the oligopolist and this is always greater than the marginal cost as the figure shows. This may lead to some selling at a slightly lower price than the agreed price, Op, and this will put pressure on the agreement and a price war may develop. This eventually leads to a competitive supply schedule.

D. Oligopolies and the Game Theory - Competition or Collusion

Game theory, developed by Von Neuman, is now applied to a variety of economic topics, such as oligopoly behaviour and international trade theory, etc. Game theory attempts to analyse oligopolists' behaviour in terms of a game where each firm tries to determine its optimal market strategy, aware that what it does will influence its competitors' behaviour, and vice versa.   An example illustrates. Assume there are two producers in a market (duopoly) and the result of each pricing strategy means a high profit when one's output is low and the others is high. How will each react to the others behaviour and what will be the result if they compete or collude? The matrix in figure 7.10 summarises the profit outcome of each firms' output decision. As the figure shows, if they both have a high output strategy, then competitive profits are £1m each. If either goes for a low output, the other firms stands to gain more profit, £3m or £2m more than a corresponding strategy of low output. However, if both pursue a selfish policy, they will return to £1m profit level outcomes each as can be seen. As shown by the solution of the Prisoners Dilemma, they would both be better off by cooperating and reducing output so that they both make £2m profit each.   This implies a cooperative policy rather than a selfish one.

Fig. 7.10 Game Theory

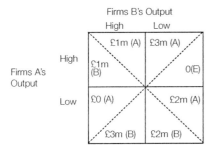

Note: £2m(A)/£2m(B) is a Nash equilibrium, when each player takes the best possible action, given the action of the other,

E. Strategic Entry Deterrence

This theory is a development of game theory whereby the incumbent firm attempts to influence the action of a would-be competitor into a market in such a way that it is favourable to the incumbent firm, for example it deters the new entrant coming into the market. These strategies cost money but if they deter the entrant they may result in extra profits.   The matrix shown in figure 7.11 outlines the alternative strategies available and the resulting profit and loss outcomes to the incumbent and would-be entrant when different decisions are taken: to come into the market or stay out , or to fight or not to fight, etc. The best strategy for the incumbent firm is if the entrant is persuaded to stay out of the market. By spending £30m on fighting and deterring the new entrant, the incumbent firm sees its profit reduced from £50m to £20m which still gives it a larger profit than any other outcomes. The worst possible situation, a fight, could be avoided with an acceptance of the new firm's entry and no deterrent imposed by the incumbent firm, but this may be an unlikely event. Strategic entry deterrence theory is also applied to multinational trade situations. Countries or companies may threaten to set up barriers to import, such as tariffs, in order to frighten off similar action by their trading partners. Ironically this may lead, in due course, to them having a stronger bargaining position in the event of tariff agreements between trading partners.

Figure 7.11 E: Strategic Entry Deterrence

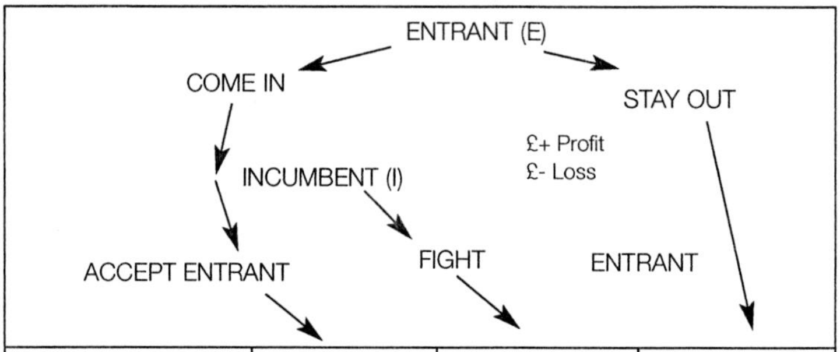

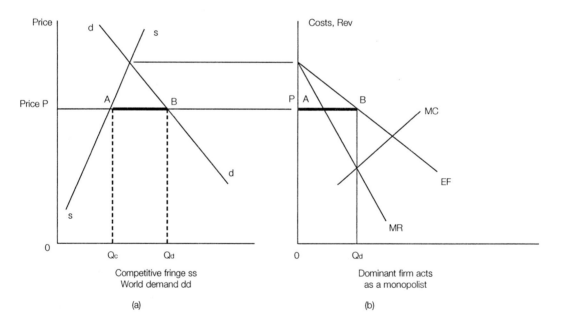

	ACCEPT ENTRANT	FIGHT	ENTRANT
Without deterrent	+10I+10E	-10I-10E	+50I 0E
With deterrent	-20I+10E	-10I-10E	+2-I 0E

Fig. 7.12 The Dominant Firm and the Competitive Fringe

The Dominant Firm and the Competitive Fringe (Post A Level)

In some markets, such as oil production, there are dominant firms co-existing with a group of competitive suppliers. This situation is illustrated in figure 7.12 (a) and (b). The competitive suppliers supply the amount ss in figure 7.12(a) so with a world demand dd, the difference between ss and dd is made up by the dominant firm who is able to determine world output and price levels since it is thus able to behave like a profit-maximising monopolist. By calculating the difference between world demand, dd, and competitive supply, the monopolist calculates a demand schedule EF, marginal revenue and marginal cost and hence the profit maximising output AB which is 0Qd. This output level allows the competitive fringe 0Qc at the monopolist price of op. In effect the dominant firm chooses the best output level and the competitive fringe supply the difference. For some low-cost competitive producers a price of Op implies a constant marginal revenue above marginal cost so they would try to increase output. However, this conflicts with the behaviour of the dominant firm so the monopolist will threaten to increase its market supply beyond 0Qd unless the fringe members control their actions. In the real world, Saudi Arabia acts as the dominant firm in setting the price of OPEC oil and other producers therefore supply the difference 0Qc.

Alternative Theories of the Firm

The assumption of profit-maximising in the business unit is possible only if managers and owners work together and there is no division between those who own and those who manage the firm. However, in the real world, in large companies, there is a difference between those who own, shareholders, and those who manage, directors, and this means it is possible for other than profit maximising objectives to be pursued. This divorce of ownership from control has led to other theories of the firm being developed and these stress managerial behaviour. The Game Theory and strategic entry deterrence has been discussed earlier (see Oligopoly Theory). We shall now examine several other theories.

Maximising Sales Revenue and Market Share

The performance of management is often rewarded financially if there is an increase in the firm's market share or sales so long as this is achieved alongside and acceptable level of profit. This allows management to buy sales by advertising which reduces profit levels and promotional costs rise. This theory of sales maximisation is associated with W. Baumol. Figure 7.13 illustrates this concept and uses the model of a profit-maximising monopolist. Profit maximising is achieved at output oq given costs and revenue. If there is some normal market level of acceptable profits, opr, then output and sales can be increased by advertising up to outputs of oq1. This level of output boosts revenue at the expense of profits. Critics of the sales maximisation theory allege that long-term profit maximising is still the objective of the firm even with short-term sales maximising and this short-term objective allows the firm to gain monopoly power in the long run in order to maximise its profit.

Fig. 7.13   Maximising Sales Revenue

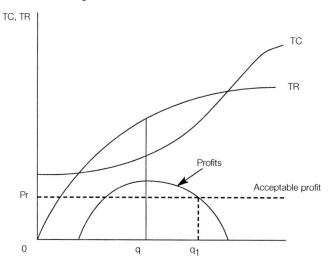

Managerial Theories of Behaviour

If shareholders are not able to control management and if the business unit operates under monopolistic conditions, then it is alleged that managers may pursue their own goals within the business. This can be such things as increasing their salaries, building up non-taxed expenses and generally increasing the size of their departments or offices or their own tax free perks, etc. This view does not refute the view that profit is the firm's objective since the more profit the manager earns for the company the more his salary increases. Nevertheless, the idea is that managers associate the growth of the company with their own self-advancement and salary performance and this management behaviour may not always be consistent with profit maximising.   Thus it could be that management will seek to increase the size of the firm but at the same time they will fight off a take-over bid by another company since this could threaten their own job, salary and status.   This could lead to a potential conflict situation between dividend policy and future management security because if dividend and share prices are high, as shareholders would wish, this will reduce the retained profits available for internal growth which ultimately benefits management.   This factor may lead to management fighting off a take-over bid which could provide not only a capital gain for shareholders, but also a guaranteed future dividend growth.

Behavioural Theories of the Firm

Management face a complexity of data and instead of maximising one particular objective, for example profit, they seek instead to achieve satisfactory levels of profits and sales over a whole range of goals. These could be satisfactory levels of profits, sales, growth, labour relations, publicity or relations with the public and government. If each of these goals are achieved then it can aspire to improve overall standards including profit levels. These are known as 'satisficing' theories of behaviour and are associated with Simon and Cyert and March. These economists took the view that the organisation could be seen as a group of conflicting interest groups such as managers, workers, creditors, shareholders and government who each have different objectives within the business unit. The organisation survives and resolves these conflicts by a process of continuous bargaining. At the micro level within the firm there also are other goals depending upon the function of the manager. These can be classified as stockholding, sales, production, credit or promotional goals. At any one time, for example the production goal is to produce as much as possible but this may be in conflict with the stock-holding goal which is to maintain economic levels of stock. As the goals conflict, compromise is needed and often a goal may be more than satisfactorily achieved, in which case there will be organisational slack, or 'excess fat' within the department. There are more resources available that are necessary to meet the current goal. This slack allows for change in the organisation without too much conflict arising because side payments can be made which allows for compromise within the organisation. These theories were developed because it was alleged that the marginalist, neoclassical, theory of the firm's behaviour, did not seem to coincide with the actual behaviour of businessmen. For one thing businessmen may not know their marginal cost or marginal revenue and furthermore it was alleged that businessmen priced on the basis of full cost plus a profit margin so that the marginalist theories used unreal assumptions and should therefore be changed to accommodate the real world. However, Machlup and Freidman still maintain the marginalist theories of the firm are still valid regardless of the reality of their assumptions. More important, they allege, is how far the neo-classical theories are able to predict testable implications about business behaviour with respect to price, output and profit: do businessmen behave as if they were seeking to maximise profits.

Galbraith's Theory of the Firm's Behaviour

Advanced by J.K. Galbraith, this theory questions the idea of consumer sovereignty in the market plact. It alleges that business units invest huge amounts of capital in new product lines and the use manipulative advertising to ensure that consumers buy their products. He supports this notion by pointing to the fact that monpolistic market structures are typical in many consumer goods industries and that little competition is really experienced. However, critics of this theory point to the failure of the Ford 'Edsel' motor car in the USA and the Strand cigarette brand in the UK where both products were heavily advertised yet proved to be failures because consumers ultimately decided they did not want to purchase them.

Contestable Markets

This is a new theory of market behaviour developed by Baumol which uses many of the traditional neo-classical ideas of the firm. The theory explains why the results associated with perfectly competitive markets can be experienced in circumstances of scale economies, usually experienced by monopolies. *Contestable* market theory explains therefore why the behaviour of monopolies can appear as if competition was present. Contestable markets are those with the following characteristics:

- there is free entry and costless exit so that any capital investment can be fully realised in the event of bankruptcy;
- there are no perceived differences in terms of the product sold in the market;
- price taking behaviour is not necessary and this is a critical difference between competitive and non-competitive market behaviour.

In essence contestable markets provide the basis for hit and run entry (competition conditions) and this means incumbent firms, even monopolists, have to move towards least-cost production methods. Also price has to equal marginal cost where these prices are set by competitive conditions, and make not more than normal profits in the long run. Otherwise the fear of hit and run entrants reduces profits to zero and could even lead to the incumbent firm going out of business. Contestable market theory is useful in explaining the similarity in behaviour in both competitive and monpolistically competitive markets in the long run.

To illustrate suppose that an industry contains four firms, each with the marginal and average cost curves shown in figure 7.14. If each firm produces Oq units of output, and charges a price of OP, total output will be four times Oq, and all four firms will earn zero economic profit. Although they could attempt to collude and push up the price. They do not do so because they know that new firms would enter the market very quickly and undercut their price. Given that entrants could sell the product at a price of OP, each firm maximises its profit by producing Oq units of output and selling it at that price.

Fig.7.14: A Contestable Market

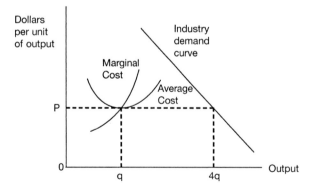

Firms in a contestable market, like those under perfect competition, will produce at lowest cost. If they produce at more than minimum cost, firms will enter the industry, produce the lower costs then the existing firms, undercut the existing firms' price, and make a profit. Thus costs will be pushed down to the lowest point. In an oligopoly, price cannot exceed marginal costs. If existing firms are charging a price in excess of marginal costs, it is profitable for an entrant to undercut the price of the existing firms.

Data Response 1

Cartels: Theory and Practice

The oil market is unlike most other commodity markets such as tea, coffee or copper. It is riddled with market imperfections. These imperfections stem from OPEC, a cartel of 13 countries which seeks to maximise the collective benefit of member states. Since 1973 OPEC has deemed it in the interest of its members to raise price considerably on two occasions (1973 and 1979), with only a marginal effect on demand.

However, with the onset of the world recession in 1980 the demand for oil was dramatically curtailed. Throughout 1984 the oil market was working strongly against OPEC and several member countries such as Nigeria and Ecuador broke ranks and produced up to 40% more oil than the agree quota. Several crisis meetings have taken place to retain the credibility and effectiveness of OPEC.

If the OPEC cartel does finally collapse this would have a severe impact on oil prices with some experts suggesting a fall in price of up to one-third. Such a price fall could have dramatic repercussions, not only for OPEC members but also for the United Kingdom and other non-OPEC oil producers.

1. Define a 'cartel' (line 3).

2. How has OPEC sought to maximise the collective benefit of member states (line 4)?

3. With reference to the text, discuss the circumstances in which a cartel might collapse.

4. Why might the price elasticity of demand for oil be different in the long run from that in the short run?

5. Explain the likely impact on the United Kingdom economy of a substantial fall in oil prices.

Data Response 2

The Rewards to an Individual Producer from Cheating on the Cartel

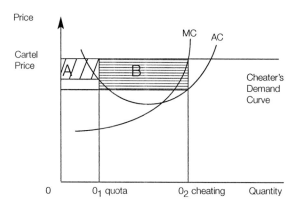

Use the figure to answer the following:

1. Why is the cartel price the same as the 'Cheaters' demand curve?

2. Why will the producer be tempted to increase production beyond Oq1?

3. Why will the 'Cheat' stop at Oq2?

4. Identify and explain the shaded areas A and B.

Data Response 3
Price Discrimination

A monopolist operates in market 1 at present and is considering also operating in market 2 with the same product. The marginal cost (MC) and revenue (MR) conditions of the two markets are shown in the diagram.

The Cost and Revenue Conditions of the Two Markets

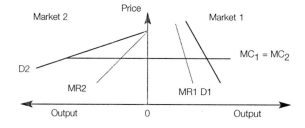

1. Under what conditions could a monopolist consider a policy of price discrimination?

2. Would you advise the monopolist to practise price discrimination in this case? Why?

3. What price would you advise him to fix in market 2? Show the profit levels in both markets.

4. Which industries practise policies of price discrimination? Why do you think they do so?

5. Compare monopolistic and competitive price, output and profit in market 1.

Data Response 4

The diagram below shows the market for parking spaces in a small country town. The only car park is owned by the local authority. There are a variety of options available to the council.

Charging for Car Parking Facilities

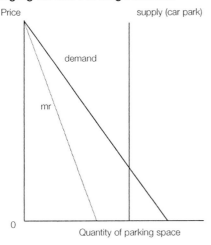

1. The council decides to provide free car parking. Show what happens in this case. (Assume there is no uncertainty on the part of potential car park users about getting a space).

2. The council wishes to ensure a free market equilibrium in order to reduce the number of motorists searching for a space.

   a) Why would they wish to do this?

   b) Show the impact of this decision on the diagram.

3. If the council decides to use ratepayers' money rather than charge users for parking, what will they do? Show it on the diagram.

4. Show the impact of a council policy designed to maximise profit with the existing car park. Outline the social costs of such a policy.

Data Response 5

The Monopolist and Competition

A monopolist, at present producing an unbranded product for the home market only, is faced by the following revenue and cost schedules.

Price	Demand	Fixed Costs	Variable Costs
20	20	200	260
18	30	200	370
16	40	200	400
14	50	200	425
12	60	200	460
10	70	200	500
8	80	200	680

1. Calculate the monopolist's equilibrium price and output.
2. Assuming the same cost condition, what would the long-run equilibrium price and output levels be if the industry were perfectly competitive? (Assume costs include normal profit).
3. Why might the cost conditions be different under perfect competition?

Data Response 6

The Monopolist and Economies of Scale

The diagram on the right shows the cost and revenue conditions of a monopolist able to exploit economies of scale, such as British Telecom

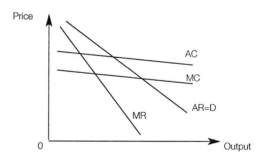

1. On a copy of the diagram, mark the output (Q1) and prices (P1) that a profit maximising commercial organisation (such as Bell in the USA) might aim for. Shade the area corresponding to profit.
2. Mark the output (Q2) and price (P2) necessary for the organisation to break even.
3. Mark the output (Q3) and price (P3) that would maximise economic efficiency. What would be the result of this pricing policy? How could the loss be covered? Who would gain, and who would lose, if the loss were covered in this way?
4. Why might the marginal cost of telephone calls decrease as shown in the diagram?
5. How does British Telecom attempt to reflect the marginal cost situation in their pricing policy? Compare this with Post Office's charges for delivering internal mail.

Data Response 7
The Publisher as a Monopolist

The diagram on the right shows the hypothetical cost and revenue conditions of a publisher operating in a monopolistic competitive market

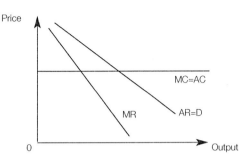

1. Explain why a book publisher may be in a 'monopolistically competitive' market.
2. The publisher attempts to maximise profits. On a copy of the diagram, show the optimum price and profit level for this.
3. The author's objective is to sell as many books as possible, since royalties are calculated as a percentage of total sales. Show where the author would wish output (and hence price) to be determined.
4. What would the price / profit situation be if the author's objectives were achieved at the expense of the publisher?
5. Assuming the diagram above is true, how would the Monopolies Commission view the situation?
6. Show the price and output that would result if copyright were abolished, and the industry became perfectly competitive. Comment on this situation.

Data Response 8
Pricing Water Supply in the Community

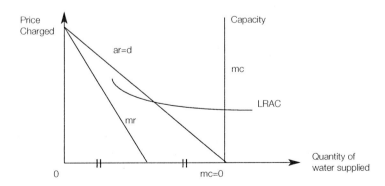

A monopolistic water authority can supply water to a community at zero marginal operating costs. The initial cost of building reservoirs and laying pipes is given by the Long Run Average Cost (LRAC). Once capacity is reached, marginal cost rises dramatically. Demand for water is given as (d). A variety of pricing options are available.

On the diagram show the price (p) and output (q) levels when the following objectives are met by the water authority.
a. Profit Maximising. Use p1/q1 and indicate the amount of profit made.
b. Break-Even in the long term. Use p2/q2.
c. Maximise economic efficiency. Use p3/q3 and briefly outline the implications of this policy.

Data Response 9

Table 1 The UK Brewing Industry 1950 - 85

Year	Total Production	Brewery Companies		Average Output per plant (thousand bulk barrels)
		No. of firms	No of plants	
1950	24.9	360	560	44
1955	24.5	320	460	53
1960	26.1	247	358	73
1965	29.9	180	274	109
1970	34.4	96	177	194
1975	39.2	82	147	167
1980	38.9	80	145	268
1985	36.5	68	117	312

Table 2 The Principal Brewery Companies in 1985

Firm	Production (million bulk barrels)	% UK Production
Bass	7.7	21.0
Allied-Lyons	4.9	13.5
Whitbread	4.4	12.0
Grand Metropolitan	4.0	11.0
Scottish and Newcastle	3.7	10.0
Courage	3.3	9.0

1. Define the meaning of each column heading and comment on the fall in number of firms 1950-85.
2. Discuss with suitable examples the economic principle at work with respect to average output per plant 1950-85.
3. What has been the pattern of total production between 1950-85? Give reasons to explain this behaviour.
4. Use table 2 to explain the market structure of brewing and discuss how you would expect the companies to behave within this structure.
5. Research and comment on the current market structure of the brewing industry.

Data Response 10

Major petrol retailers

Who gets how much from a litre of petrol

Duty	34.3p
VAT	8.15p
Production cost	8.19p
Retail margin	2.00p
Company margin	2.06p

1 litre of petrol at 54.7p

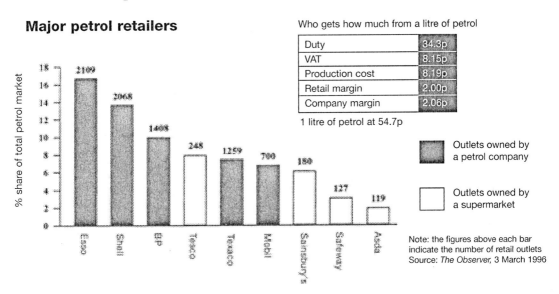

Outlets owned by a petrol company

Outlets owned by a supermarket

Note: the figures above each bar indicate the number of retail outlets
Source: *The Observer*, 3 March 1996

1. Which market structure best describes petrol retailing? Justify your answer.

2. BP and Mobil announced plans to merge their petrol retailing operations in 1996. Examine *two* possible reasons for their decision.

3. Many of the oil companies own petrol outlets.
    (a) What type of intergration best describes this situation?
    (b) Examine the effects of this form of intergration.

4. There has been an increase in the number of supermarket chains selling petrol in the UK in recent years.
    (a) Calculate the proportion of outlets selling petrol accounted for by the four supermarket chains.
    (b) Analyse the effects of the entry of supermarkets into the retail petrol market.

Multiple Choice

1. The practice of 'charging what the traffic will bear' is:
   a. a form of discriminating monopoly
   b. a policy confined to the telephone calls
   c. adopted when fixed cost is spread over the greater quantity of output.

2. A monopolist, incurring fixed costs but with zero variable costs, maximises his total profit at a level of output at which :
   a. marginal revenue is positive
   b. point elasticity of demand is positive approaching unity
   c. total revenue is maximised.

3. In the long run, a profit maximising firm under conditions of perfect competition produces an output at which:
   a. average revenue equals marginal cost
   b. average cost equals marginal revenue
   c. average revenue equals average cost.

4. The main difference between the oligopolistic market and that of monopolistic competition is that under oligopoly:
   a. there is no competition through advertising
   b. there is product differentiation
   c. there are few sellers, each with a sizeable proportion of the market
   d. the firms will earn super-normal profits
   e. the firms can aim at profit maximisation.

5. Where a few large firms dominate the market, barriers to the entry of other firms into the market are not uncommon. One of the following is unlikely to be applied:
   a. existing firms restrict the new entrant's share of the market by increasing the number of similar but differentiated products made by each firm
   b. 'fighting companies' can be established specially to undercut the new entrant in its market
   c. existing firms can increase the strength of their advertising
   d. where economies of scale exist the individual firm may be large enough to ensure lower unit costs than the necessarily small new entrant, and the cost differential will be a barrier.

6. An oligopolist:
   a. needs to consider how competitors will react to any price change
   b. is not concerned with competitors since there are so few of them
   c. must always attempt to maximise profits or be eliminated
   d. does not have to be concerned about either marginal or average cost.

7. If all sellers in a market are known to be charging the same price which one of the following statements about market structure and behaviour is correct?
    a. the market is perfectly competitive
    b. the market is perfectly oligopolistic
    c. the price is determined collusively
    d. the price is set by a price leader.

8. Which of the following conditions are necessary for price discrimination to be possible and profitable?
    a. imperfect competition, including monopoly, exists in the market
    b. the market is capable of division into different price elasticities of demand
    c. costs of maintaining market divisions are low in relation to benefits arising from elasticity differences
    d. there are different costs for supplying different markets.

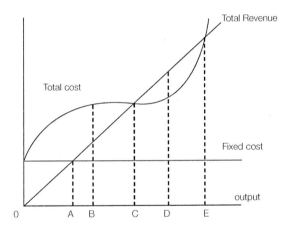

9. The above diagram shows the cost and revenue situation of a firm. If the firm increases output from OD to OE which of the following is incorrect?
    a. the firm moves to the long run perfectly competitive output level
    b. the firm is a member of a price-fixing cartel
    c. the firm is a profit-maximising monopolist in equilibrium
    d. the firm is a nationalised industry attempting to break even
    e. none of the above statements is incorrect.

10. Which of the following is the least likely characteristic of an oligopolistic situation in industry?
    a. co-operation, overt or tacit, between firms
    b. competition in service and/or quality of product
    c. the domination of the industry by a few large firms
    d. 'cut-throat' price competition
    e. some differentiation of product.

chapter eight

Government and Markets - Monopolies - Mergers

The Economic Justification for Intervention (See fig 8.1)

Assuming constant long-run costs (LMC = LAC) in a competitive industry, the price / ouput levels are opc/oqc and overall economic efficiency is maximised as price = marginal cost = long-run average cost. If the structure of industry became monopolistic, initially in the form a cartel, price and output levels change to opm/oqm and inefficiency arises in the form of the dead-weight loss, triangle a, where price (pm) exceeds marginal cost. Otherwise the higher price and profits, area b, represent a transfer of resources from consumers to producers and factors of production. The higher price and profits together with lower output under monopolistic conditions provide the theoretical justification for intervention in the market. There are two approaches possible, namely to control or regulate the conduct of the monopolist or to influence the structure of the monopolistic industry by breaking it up into smaller competitive units or by functionally separating its ability to operate in different markets.

Regulation of Monopoly Conduct

The government, or regulatory body, can induce a competitive price/output level by subsidising costs so that MC = MR at an output/price level consistent with a competitive market structure, i.e. costs fall to LMC2, LAC2 and price/output are at opm2, oqm2. Even so critics argue that this policy will still create a monopoly profit and the lower price is paid by the tax payer.

Fig. 8.1 Competitive v Monopolistic Industries

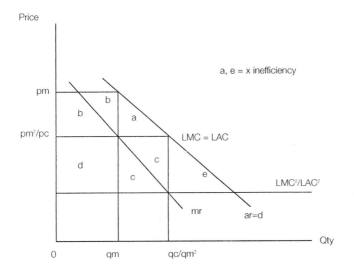

The government can impose a competitive price/output level or leave the monopolist to set a price and then tax away any excess profits. However, this policy presumes (i) the government knows the competitive price/output level and, anyway, (ii) the monopolist can artificially inflate costs so any profits disappear and there is therefore, nothing to tax.

The government can encourage competitively priced imports into the country so the monopolist has to reduce price and increase output to a more competitive level.

Changing the Structure of the Industry

The government can encourage new entrants into a monopolistic industry by reducing barriers to entry. This would mean the abolition of patent or copyright laws protecting existing firms, the limiting of advertising expenditure, the outlawing of restrictive practices in both product and factor markets and an insistence upon competitive codes of practice being pursued by the monopolist.

The government can actively encourage overseas imports (see above) as well as attracting overseas capital, i.e. providing other suppliers of the product. A free trade policy within the international economy would also have a similar result.

Where state-owned monopolies, e.g. nationalised Industries, exist these should be open to competitive pressures such as privatisation and deregulation.

Mergers and Economies of Scale

When mergers exist in an industry, so creating multiplant operations, then long-run economies of scale arise which lower costs, i.e. LMC2/LAC2 in Fig. 8.1. This leads to price and output levels consistent with competitive markets, i.e. pm2, qm2. Monopoly profits are still made (areas c plus d). In this case the gains in profit are achieved through economies so costs reduce. The only inefficiency is that there is a theoretical loss of consumer surplus equivalent to the triangle e. However, the cost reduction, areas d plus c, means that these resources are released and can be used elsewhere in the economy.

UK Monopoly and Mergers Policy and Control

Government Regulatory Agencies

Monopolies and Mergers Commission (MMC)

The MMC (established in 1948) can investigate any local or national dominant firm which has 25% or more of the market. The investigation seeks to establish whether the monopoly operates 'against the public interest'. A pragmatic approach is adopted and such things as whether there are substitutes available in the market for the public, the level of profits earned to capital employed by the monopolist, the level of technical innovation in the monopolistic industry, as well as potential methods of reducing entry barriers in order to encourage future competition, are investigated. The MMC has reported on over fifty monopoly situations which have covered such things as brick production, film processing, drug pricing, breakfast cereals and the instant coffee market (1991), etc. In 1989 it reported on the UK brewing industry and recommended that the industry adopt a more competitive structure by advising that the brewers sell off some of their pubs and also suggesting that 'guest' beers be introduced into the brewers' tied houses. Nevertheless, throughout its history the MMC has not generally been overly critical of those monopolies investigated. At the same time, the often inconsistent behaviour of the MMC with respect to merger policy has led some to suggest that in a take-over situation the predatory company should have to show the bid was in the public interest which may be more difficult to prove than merely not being against the public interest.

Restrictive Trade Practices Court

This court (established in 1956) together with the Registrar of Restrictive Practices, investigates restrictive practices such as collusive price and restrictive conditions of sale agreements. It assumes these are illegal unless it can be proved they are justified by one of the eight 'gateways' which show they may be beneficial to the public interest. These are listed below:

- the agreement is necessary to protect the public against injury;
- the agreement ensures that the public receives some specific and substantial benefit which would disappear if the agreement were ended;
- the agreement is necessary to enable small firms to compete with large firms;
- the agreement is necessary to prevent small firms being exploited by very large customers or suppliers;
- the agreement is necessary to maintain the level of employment in particular areas or industries;
- the agreement is necessary to maintain exports;
- the agreement is necessary to maintain another restriction already approved by the court.

Even if an agreement satisfies one of these points, it must still be shown that the benefit from it outweighs any general detriment to the public from the agreement as a whole.

The Fair Trading Act 1973 transferred responsibility for the control of restrictive practices to the Director General of Fair Trading, and at the same time brought the provision of services within the same framework of control. As a tidying-up process, the various aspects of the policy were pulled together in the Restrictive Practices Act 1977.

Over 5,000 restrictive practice agreements had been registered by the late 1980s and the vast majority had been outlawed and disbanded. In terms of figure 8.1 restrictive practices operate as if they were monopolies, with a price output of opm/oqm, but they have none of the corresponding economies of scale associated with large scale monopolistic production.

Merger Policy - Monopolies and Mergers Act 1973

The strong movement towards market and output concentration in the UK since the war has led to a rise in the five firm concentration ratio, CR5, in manufacturing industries and, recently, the growth of conglomerate holdings. The Monopolies and Mergers Act of 1973 amended the 1965 Act and allowed investigation, and hence recommendation to the relevant government minister, with respect to allowing a proposed merger. A merger could be investigated if: it leads to an increase in monopoly power (25% or more of the market share) and hence, a reduction in consumer choice, or where gross assets after the merger exceed £38 million. The onus is on the investigation proving the 'guilt' of the merger in terms of it being against the public interest and this in practice is difficult to show. Few large mergers have been prevented. In the event that the MMC concludes, by a greater than two-thirds majority, that the proposed merger is against the public interest, then the merger is not allowed to proceed.

The Rationale for Merger Policy (some views)

The free-trade view is to allow all mergers to take place since the reason why one firm wishes to buy another is that the acquiring firm believes it can run the acquired firm more profitably than its existing owners. This treat of take-over makes all firms operate efficiently and when mergers take place resources move from less profitable to more profitable uses. The implication is that policy should be non-interventionist regardless of likely social or political implications.

The cost-benefit approach is to compare the likely cost gains of a merger and weigh them against the loss of choice and consumer surplus. A horizontal merger would lead to cost savings, in figure 8.1 shown as the areas (d+c), due to greater economies of scale. However, competitor pressures might have reduced the price so consumers could lose the area e, in the form of consumer surplus. However, this assumes a non-merged industry could keep costs and prices below opm2.

The interventionist stance is that mergers should be closely monitored because of the impact on industrial structure and the possibility of regional unemployment resulting from mergers. Furthermore it is argued that pre- and post-merged industries do not show significant profitability changes so the commercial efficiency of mergers has not been proven. Evidence seems to suggest whilst profitability does not result from mergers monopoly, control over markets certainly does.

The Impact of UK Merger Policy

During the period from the introduction of the merger policy to the end of 1984, a total of 2,565 proposed mergers was examined by the Mergers Panel as falling within the scope of the policy. Of these proposed mergers, 79 were referred to the MMC for further investigation (and this includes seven cases where two or more bids for a single firm were referred). Amongst those referred to the MMC, 23 have been abandoned during the MMC investigations so that the MMC has not finally reported. Of those proposed mergers on which the MMC had reported by 1986, 23 were found to be against the public interest and 32 not against the public interest. Thus the direct impact of the merger policy can be seen to be rather small: only 1 - 2% of all proposed mergers have been stopped.

Consumer Protection Acts

Fair Trading Act 1973

This Act created the post of Director General of Fair Trading under whom all competition and consumer law was centralised. Consumer protection was provided under this Act in such areas as insurance, hire purchase and house purchase. The Director General could prohibit practices which adversely affect consumers inthe market place.

Competition Act 1980

This was designed to stimulate competition and this Act was extended to Nationalised Industries. The Director General of Fair Trading could refer price rises and practices of Nationalised Industries to the MMC which was empowered to investigate in order to see whether the Nationalised Industry acted against the public interest.

Nationalisation, Privatisation and Deregulation

The 1980s saw a radical programme of government action in the industrial sphere. This programme had three policy objectives:

- to privatise nationalised industries and re-regulate where necessary;
- to deregulate controlled industries;
- to subject state agencies to competitive price tender.

These policies were designed to improve competition within the state run sectors of the economy.

The Economics of Nationalisation

The nationalisation programme started after the second World War (1945) with the public ownership of coal, gas, electricity and rail etc. The basic economic rationales for nationalisation were :

- To provide the huge capital injections required to gain economies of scale in key industrial sectors. Immediately after the was it was felt the private sector was unable to generate the required investment in the basic energy and transport industries and only state provision and funding was feasible under these circumstances.

■ By owning monopolies the state could regulate their conduct and performance, i.e. non-profit-maximising price and monopoly output levels could be pursued by state owned industries. This would enable the state to pursue non-profit maximising objectives such as levels of service, equality of opportunity and other social objectives. In terms of figure 8.1 any combination of price and output levels could be agreed upon, e.g. in particular, opc/oqc so that the maximisation of economic efficiency, with price (p) = marginal cost (mc), was theoretically achievable. Not only does p= mc level ensure allocative efficiency but it also stops monopoly exploitation which would result if private enterprise existed.

Problems of Marginal Cost Pricing in Nationalised Industries

Where industries were nationalised in order to achieve economic efficiency by setting price to marginal cost certain problems were encountered:

■ How to define the marginal unit? In order to work out marginal cost, it is necessary to be clear about the units produced . In terms of railway services, is the unity the train, or the carriage, or the extra seat?

■ Furthermore it is difficult and expensive to estimate the charge the marginal cost of the last train since there are practical problems of costing fixed and variable costs.

■ Many nationalised industries are faced by daily and seasonal fluctuations in demand so making it difficult to identify and charge the actual marginal cost for the good provided; the electricity industry is a case in point.

■ In some industries short and long-run marginal cost differences exist so there are problems of which one to choose, with respect to pricing policies.

■ Marginal cost pricing can lead to losses in natural monopoly situations. See below

Nationalisation and Natural Monopolies

The strongest reason for nationalisation was based on the view that many industries were natural monopolies which needed strict control through state ownership and which thus allowed the state to exploit potential economies of scale. A natural monopoly is one where one firm is so efficient that its costs of production preclude the possibility of competition by other firms. This is because the single firm experiences cost falls over its entire output range. A single firm can produce the total output at a lower unit cost than can two or more firms sharing that industry output amongst them. Thus natural market forces lead to the emergence of one large firm, i.e. a natural monopoly. This is illustrated in figure 8.2 . A single firm industry has costs as shown and is producing at oq1, with costs of Oc1 and a price of P1. Two firms in the industry could produce Oq2, each, i.e. half Oq1, at a cost of c2 and price of OP2. These costs and price are higher than those of the single firm. Thus the single firm can produce the total output of Oq1, at a lower price of OP1 which is lower than the cost oc2 of either of the two potential entrants. In the case of electricity or gas supply such economies of scale exist which was one reason why these industries were nationalised.

Natural Monopolies and Financial Losses

Allocative efficiency requires that price be set to marginal cost. In the case of a natural monopoly, in figure 8.2 the price/output level of op3/oq3 implies a price less than average cost, i.e. a loss for the nationalised industry. This means long-term investment will not produce a commercial return on capital employed and will appear to be commercially uneconomic. The industry is nationalised and the loss paid by the taxpayer.

Fig. 8.2 A Natural Monopolist

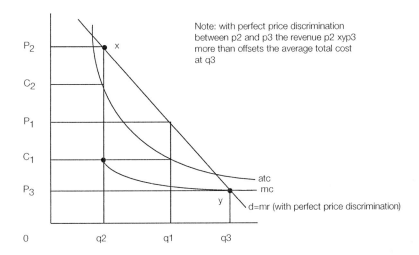

Note: with perfect price discrimination between p2 and p3 the revenue p2 xyp3 more than offsets the average total cost at q3

Social Justice

An industry should not only be owned by those who can afford to buy shares but by all in society. Also nationalisation helps maintain national defence interests and by nationalising coal, etc. it helped the government control the economy more easily and establish minimum safety standards underground.

Criticisms of Nationalised Industries - Privatisation

The problem of pricing within the nationalised industries led to charges of inadequate and uncertain investment, a poor return on capital, less choice and quality of service, accompanied by strong trades unions with featherbedding and subsidies which wasted taxpayers' money. It was alleged that a more competitive market structure was needed to force costs and prices down. Following the 1979 Conservative Government, a policy of privatisation was pursued whereby state industries were sold off to the public in return for ordinary shares. The list below shows the current position of those industries which were privatised along with existing nationalised industries as well as deregulated industries - see table 8.1.

The following industries have been privatised since 1979:

British Rail

British Telecom

British Gas Corporation

Electricity (England and Wales)

North of Scotland Hydro-Electric Board

South of Scotland Electricty Board

British National Oil Corporation

British Airways

British Airports Authority

British Aerospace

Water (England and Wales)

British Shipbuilders (Warships)

British Steel Corporation

British Transport Docks Board

National Freight Company

Enterprise Oil

National Bus Company

Table 8.1 Deregulation	Long-distance buses. Real fare reduction of 40% 1980-83.
Transport Act (1980)	Urban bus service.
Transport Act (1986) Health and Social Security Act (1984)	Abolition of opticians' monopoly in dispensing and selling spectacles.
	'Big Bang' Abolition of solicitors' monopoly on property conveyancing.
	Charges down 25%.
Stock Exchange agreement Financial Services Act (1986)	Abolition of wage, price and foreign exchange controls (1979)

The Competition Act 1998 (Effect 1st March 2000)

General Points

The latest statement on competition in the EU is contained in the Competition Act of 1998 as shown below:-

- It is estimated that cartels can add up to 10% on prices of both industrial and consumer goods in the UK.

- The total cost of anti-competitive practises and the abuse of market power is estimated to be several billion pounds (around 1% of the UK's GDP).

- It has been argued that the main weakness in UK law was the lack of 'bite', i.e. inadequate powers of investigation coupled with weak penalties, and poorly drafted legislation which often concentrated on the form of agreements rather than their commercial significance.

- The UK has adopted, with minor variations, the regime that operates across the European Union for abuses that effect trade between the member states - in particular Articles 81 and 82 of the Treaty of Rome. This is partly part of the process of harmonisation that is intended to free up barriers to trade between member countries.

- It is generally recognised that the European model has been more effective in suppressing abuses.

- The new act focuses more on the economic impact of agreements and practises that prevent, restrict or distort competition, as well as those that are intended to.

- They can be made by individual firms or trade associations and can be attempts to restrict prices or levels of production or sales.

Competition Policy Up-date

The Competition Act 1998 (effective 1 March 2000): the Main Points

- Agreements that distort, restrict or prevent competition, or are intended to, are outlawed.
- The Office of Fair Trading receives greater powers, including the ability to carry out dawn raids, seize documents and order a halt to restrictive practises.
- Fines are increased to a maximum of 10% of UK turnover for up to 3 years.
- Fines can be mititgated for organisations that have an effective compliance programme.
- Whistleblowers reporting cartels of which they are members will be completely exempt from punishment.
- The act only applies to offences committed after March 2000.
- Monopolies and Mergers is now re-named as the Competition Commission.
- The Competition Act 1998 effective from 1 March 2000 is:

  an Act to make provision about competition and the abuse of a dominant position in the market; to confer powers in relation to investigations conducted in connection with Article 85 or 86 of the treaty establishing the European Community; to ammend the Fair Trading Act 1973 in relation to information which may be required in connection with investigations under that Act; to make provision with respect to meaning of 'supply of services' in the fair trading Act 1974; and for connected purposes.

- One of the main effects of the Act is to bring UK competition policy into line with EU policy, hence the compliance with Articles 85 and 86 of the European Commission.
- Chapter 1 of the Competition Act introduces two broad 'prohibitions' similar to those used by the European Commission to control commercial arrangements which may affect trade within the UK and which prevents, restricts or distorts competition in the UK to an appreciable extent - or is intended to have that effect. Examples might be arrangements to fix prices or to share out markets.
- The Chapter 2 prohibition makes it unlawful for companies to abuse a dominant market position, for example by imposing unfair purchase or selling prices or by applying different trading conditions to equivalent transactions in a way that puts some parties at a competitive disadvantage. whether a firm is in a dominant position will depend to large extent on the structure of the market in

question, but a general rule it is unlikely to be considered dominant if its market share is less than 40%. (Note that this is not merger legislation but restrictive practices).

- Companies infringing the Act face a number of possible consequences, including:
- agreements being void and unenforceable
- investigation by the OFT (Office of Fair Trading)
- a financial penalty of up to 10% of UK turnover
- the possibility of being sued for damages by those harmed by the
- unlawful agreement or conduct.

The Costs of Government Regulation

Many argue that excessive government regulation in factor and product markets can be costly because :-

a   regulators may not know the correct economic standards of output or price and attempts to ascertain these can be expensive and lead to a waste of resources;

b   legal controls imposed can push up costs of production which mean consumers pay more than they want or should have to pay. Bureaucratic costs also have to be paid by producer and/or consumer (see below);

c   taxation and subsidies distort factor resource allocation because they provide the wrong price signals to producers, consumers and income earners.

d   politicians can interfere in markets in order to gain votes. Public choice economics argues that regulation is a product which is bought and sold like any other good. Regulations, e.g. import controls, feathered home producers at the expense of cheaper import prices for the consumer;

e   the regulators often rely upon the regulated industry for the information which enables them to supposedly exercise regulatory control. However, this over dependency by the regulator leads to "regulatory capture" so the regulatory authority is unable to exercise objective control on behalf of the consumer;

f   the development of Public Choice economics stresses that the bureaucratic cost of regulation outweighs the benefits.

g   of directly unproductive profit seeking (D.U.P.). This area of economics analyses the ways of profit seeking that do not directly contribute to the output of an economy's goods and services. A government is a monopoly provider of goods, services, taxation, regulation, etc. and within this situation bureaucratic and lobby interests develop because monopoly profits can result from government action. Safety regulations can increase the profits of seat belt manufacturers and tax avoidance schemes provide income for accountants and other professionals. Professional lobbyists sell their services in order to convince government bureaucrats of regulation in certain areas so wasteful costs can arise, e.g. lobbying to encourage governments to place a tariff on an imported good means consumers pay more and producers gain monopoly profits. Many argue that in order to reduce D.U.P. and hence its associated wastes, governments should devolve more power to its citizens who are the only impartial or non-biased agency with respect to the general interest of all citizens. This means markets make the decisions and the lobby costs of vested interests would appear.

h   since commercial control of monopolies, using regulatory agencies, was seen to be expensive, in particular with respect to Nationalised Industries, it was argued the cheapest course of action would be to introduce competition, i.e. self-regulation by a privatisation process which would loosen up markets. In its most extreme this view argues that governments should reduce all artificial entry barriers to an industry, e.g. abolish patens and copyrights and, where externalities exist, allow each party to the externality free negotiation rights rather than pursuing a government policy of taxation or regulatory control, i.e. allow markets to determine the outcome (internalise the situation).

Data Response 1

The Economics of Regulating Markets

There have been numerous examples of regulation. They have included employment legislation embracing contracts; employment protection; equal opportunities; health and safety at work and training and redundancy. At various times there have been controls on prices, wages and profits in such forms as minimum wages; equal pay; rent control; price regulation schemes (for example NHS drugs); profit rules on government contracts; and price freezes for the nationalised industries. The structure, conduct and performance of industry has been regulated by monopolies, mergers and restrictive practices policy. Regulation has also taken the form of government licensing of entry as with patents; public houses; taxis; television companies; road and air transport; and new pharmaceutical products. Finally market output is regulated through such forms as pollution controls and safety standards, as in the case of food products and passenger transport.

Market regulation involves substantial transaction costs in negotiating, monitoring and enforcing regulatory rules. Staff are needed by the regulatory agency and costs are imposed on producers in responding to the regulator's requirements. For example, a monopoly inquiry involves substantial inputs by members of the inquiry team and corresponding inputs by the monopolist. Specialist witnesses will also be hired by both parties, and the monopolist might devote resources to a public relations campaign and to lobbying politicians.   There are also possible indirect costs which need to be included in the analysis. For example, regulatory requirements for the introduction of new drugs into the NHS might lead to longer development periods, so delaying the introduction of new pharmaceutical products. There might also be adverse effects on innovation with fewer new drugs being marketed, and firms might shift their R & D activities to foreign locations where there are fewer regulatory restrictions. In the meantime, delays in the introduction of new drugs can have harmful effects on patients in the form of prolonged suffering and death which might have been avoided by the earlier use of the new product.

A cost-benefit analysis of regulation must also take account of its potential benefits. Regulatory agencies which aim to remove market failures will introduce policies to correct for externalities or to change the structure, conduct or performance of markets with the ultimate objective of improving consumer welfare. But can society assess the output or performance of a regulatory agency? Various performance indicators have been suggested, not all of which can be easily related to consumer satisfaction. For example, agencies are likely to emphasise the number of inquiries and reports; the number licences issued, the number of inspections; the number of prosecutions; and the size of the regulatory authority.

Source: C.S.O.

1. Outline the main reasons and methods for market regulation.

2. Discuss how cost-benefit analysis could be used to discuss alternatives to regulating pollution from a cement works.

Data Response 2 (Water Supplies)

In the UK, where adequate water supplies have been taken for granted, the situation is changing. A number of dry winters and summer droughts have resulted in restrictions on the consumption of water.

As well as the effects of natural influences, there have been alterations to the structure andand operation of the water industry. Water, which was formerly supplied by government authorities, is now provided by private sector companies.

The traditional charging system for households has been based on the value of the house, not on the amount of water used. While this is still the case for many homes, new houses are likely to have water meters so that payment for water depends mainly upon the amount consumed. At present, the UK has 5% of homes with water meters, in contrast to Germany and Finland where there is 100% metering.

1. Explain **two** reasons for water being supplied by government authorities rather than private sector companies.

2. Discuss whether water meters should be installed in more UK homes.

chapter nine

Aggregate Demand and Supply

Understanding Macro-Economic problems

Supply and demand analysis can also be used to explain and analyse macro-economic problems such as inflation and unemployment. Aggregate supply is total output which is also a measure of employment and hence unemployment. Aggregate demand represents the whole demand in an economy. When the two are combined problems of inflation and unemployment can be easily understood and government policy can be applied and evaluated. Aggregate demand and supply are now outlined.

Aggregate Demand

Aggregate demand is the total demand in the economy made up of spending by households, firms and the goverment, plus exports and minus imports of the overseas sector, i.e. C+I+G+(X-M).

The Aggregate Demand Curve

The aggregate demand curve (AD) is plotted against the price level on the vertical axis and real national income (i.e. real GDP) on the horizontal axis. See figure 9.1.

The Slope of the Curve

The AD curve is downward sloping showing that at higher price levels the total demand for goods and services in the economy is likely to be lower. The reasons for this are:

- As the price level rises, real wealth falls and therefore less is spent.

- As the price level rises, UK goods become less competitive both at home and abroad, therefore spending on UK goods falls - exports go down and imports go up.
- As the price level rises, interest rates also tend to rise and therefore dampen down interest-sensitive expenditures such as investment by firms and consumption of luxuries and consumer durables by households.

Fig. 9.1

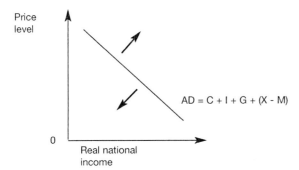

It is important to distinguish between a shift of the curve and a movement along the curve. In this case a movement along wil be caused by a change in the price level whereas a shift of the curve will be caused by a change in factors other than a change in the price level.

Shifts of the Curve

An increase in aggregate demand is shown by a shift of the curve to the right, whereas a fall is shown by a shift to the left. This may be due to the following circumstances.

A change in autonomous expenditure

If, for example, businesses decide to invest more because they feel more optimistic about the prospects for the economy, this will cause more spending at each and every price level and therefore a shift of the AD curve to the right. If, they take the view that prospects look gloomy, and decide to postpone investment, this will cause the curve to shift to the left. If households decide to save more (perhaps because they fear unemploymet), this will also cause the curve to shift to the left. (The consumption function shows the relationship between the income of households or consumers, and their spending. When households save a bigger proportion of their income, the propensity to consume falls.)

The extent of the level of saving is measured by the income multiplier. The more saving and less consumption the smaller the multiplier and vice versa. If the multiplier is large then the aggregate demand shift will be large after the initial injection of spending. A rise in the propensity to save will reduce the size of the multiplier and even send it into reverse, i.e. negative. Hence the aggregate demand curve will shift to the left.

Changes in interest rates

A fall in interest rates will lead to an increase in interest-sensitive expenditures at each and every price level by both firms and households. This will shift the AD curve to the right.

Changes in disposable income

Disposable income is income after tax. If the government raises taxes on income, this will cause a fall in aggregate demand at each and every price level and thus cause the AD curve to shift to the left, i.e. government spending net of taxation. Changes in world demand or trade will also affect the level of disposable income.

Aggregate Supply

The aggregate supply curve (AS) shows how the total output of an economy varies with changes in the price level. The following will affect the shape of the aggregate supply curve:

- the degree of competition between firms
- factor mobility
- wage bargaining procedures
- the extent to which costs vary with output.

The Slope of the Curve

The single most important factor affecting the shape or slope of the AS curve is how close the economy is to its potential, or full employment, output.

In figure 9.2, the horizontal part of the curve relates to where an increase in output can be achieved without an increase in the price level. This is most likely to happen when there is substatial unemployment of resources (unemployed labour and excess capital capacity) and firms can increase their output without having to pay higher prices of production.

The upward sloping part of the supply curve shows that the price level increases as well as output and employment. The additional resources required to increase output can be obtained by firms only at higher prices than previously. To compensate for their higher costs firms require higher prices for their output and bottlenecks will occur in production.

The vertical part of the supply curve shows what happens when resources are fully employed. This is the limit to which output can be expanded. This limit exists because of the limits to the size and quality of the workforce, the amount of capital stock and the rate of return on the investment of capital stock. In theory it is possible to increase output by extending the working week, reducing the school leaving age, raising the retirement age, using factories 24 hours a day with a shift system and so on. But in practice there are limits to the amount of extra hours firms can operate their plant and equipment (because of costly wear and tear and breakdowns). Once these limits have been reached, further increases in the price level have no effect upon output.

Fig. 9.2

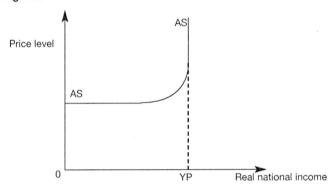

Short-Run and Long-Run Supply

A distinction can be made between the short-run and the long-run aggregate supply curve. In the short run, when output can be increased, the curve is horizontal or positively sloped. In the long run, the limit to output having been reached, the curve is vertical.

Shifts of the Curve

Figure 9.3 shows a change in the economy's productive capacity. Y_p1 is the maximum potential output of the economy with given resources and state of technology. Thus economic growth is represented by a movement of AS to the right (AS1-AS2) with a corresponding increase in Yp (Y_p1-Y_p2). A loss of resources (e.g. worn out capital not being replaced) would be represented as a movement to the left (AS1-AS3). Other supply side factors that could cause such shifts include:

- changes in the tax laws which affect incentives
- a change to the school leaving age
- a change in the retirement age.

Fig. 9.3

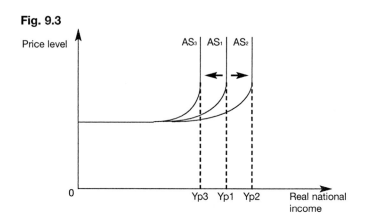

Integrating Aggregate Demand and Supply

Equilibrium national income

Figure 9.4 shows that with aggregate demand (AD) and aggregate supply (AS), the equilibrium level of real national income would be Y_E. Applied to an actual economy, Y_E would show:

- the value of goods and services produced in a given period
- the rewards or incomes generated by this production
- the expenditure on goods and services
- the level of employment.

Fig. 9.4 Equilibrium national income

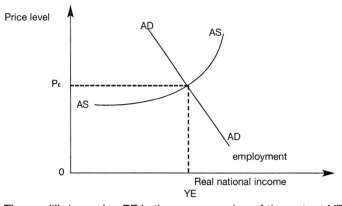

The equilibrium price PE is the average price of the output YE. Producers are willing to supply, and purchasers to buy, *this* output at *this* price.

A change in equilibrium output, in GDP, might occur because of a change in either aggregate demand or aggregate supply.

Fig. 9.5. The affect of aggregate demand increases with aggregate supply unchanged.

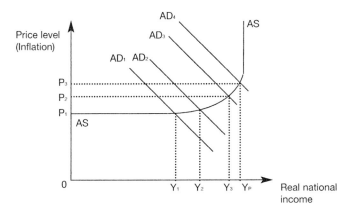

Changes in Aggregate Demand: impact on unemployment and inflation

The precise effect of a change in aggregate demand, on the equilibrium price and on output levels, depends upon the slope of the aggregate supply curve over the range affected. Figure 9.5 shows that if the AD curve shifts to the right in the horizontal range of the AS curve (AD1-AD2) then the entire effect will be on the level of output (an increase in real national income), with the price level staying the same. Over this range there are plenty of under-utilized resources, including unemployed labour and capital, because demand for these resources is so low. This type of unemployment is known as demand-deficient unemployment. An increase in demand under these conditions (as, for example, in the Great Depression of the 1930s) is unlikely to cause price rises (i.e. inflation).

If aggregate demand increases over the upward sloping part of the curve (AD2 to AD3) then the effect will be on both price level *and* output. This is because, as the economy picks up, some firms will have reached or be getting close to capacity output, and shortages of certain factors of production, such as skilled labour and raw materials, will begin to develop.

This will cause prices to rise, and so inflationary pressure will start building up. If aggregate demand *continues* to rise (AD3 to AD4), as most firms reach their maximum potential output the effect will be mainly on the price level. Eventually firms reach their productive limit (at which point AS is vertical) and they would be unable to increase output further in response to further increases in aggregate demand. In this situation any increase in AD is only reflected in higher prices. When prices rise in these conditions it is referred to as demand-pull inflation.

Inflation can also be caused by increases in the costs of production. The following items can push up production costs, i.e costs push inflation.

- **Wages and salaries.** A wage-price spiral can occur where wages rise, prices are pushed up, workers demand more wages to compensate and prices rise again.
- **Prices of imported goods.** As a major importer of raw materials the UK is affected by the value of the pound.
- **Profits.** Firms can decide to raise their profit margins.
- Too much money can also cause prices to rise.

A change in the costs of raw materials, labour or capital will lead to a change in the prices at which firms are prepared to sell their output. An increase in costs will raise the aggregate supply curve vertically. A fall in costs will shift it to the right.

Fig. 9.6

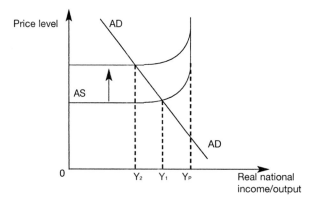

The effect of an increase in costs, with aggregate demand is shown in figure 9.6.

Government fiscal and monetary policy can be reflationary or deflationary which will shift aggregate demand to the right or left respectively. Supply side policies are designed to make the economy more competitive so costs fall and the aggregate supply schedule shifts to the right. This was the basis of the 'Thatcherite' revolution of the 1980s, although real income shifts seem to have been stimulated via demand policies e.g. cuts in interest rates and taxation rather than by supply shifts to the right.

The Long-Run Aggregate Supply Schedule (LAS)

Fig. 9.7

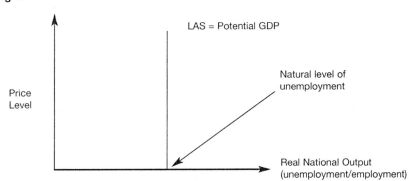

The long-run aggregate supply schedule (LAS), shows the relationship between potential output (GDP) in real terms and full employment, i.e. the natural level of unemployment figure 9.7. Real output is independent of the price level so the LAS is vertical and can only move as the potential output of the economy, capacity increases or decreases. Thus changing the long-term 'natural level of unemployment'.

The Phillips Curve

The Phillips Curve (see figure 9.8) shows the inverse relationship between the unemployment rate and the rate of inflation. Hence if the government wants to reduce unemployment, from 6% to 3%, inflation will go up from 5% to 10% or vice versa. The Phillips Curve therefore shows the 'trade-off' the government will have to accept in order to achieve their macro-economic policy objective of, for example, reducing unemployment.

Fig. 9.8

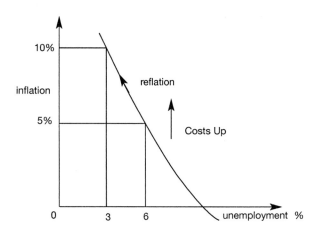

The Long Run Aggregate Supply Schedule (LAS) and the Phillips Curve

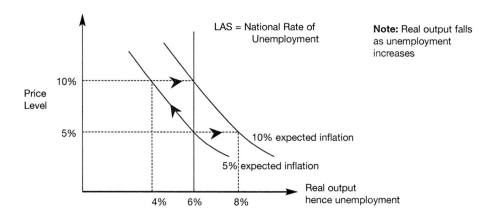

See Fig. 9.9

In figure 9.9 there are two short run Phillips curves representing two rates of expected inflation, i.e. 5% and 10% . If the expected equals the actual rate of 5% then unemployment will be at the long run rate, i.e. the natural rate of 6%. If the actual rate of inflation is 10%, after reflation, then the economy will experience 4% unemployment with expected inflation of 5% in the short term, i.e. the economy moves along the 5% Phillips curve. However, firms will now experience inflationary wage claims above productivity levels and will cut back their labour demands until the economy moves back to a 6% unemployment level. Here the 10% Phillips curve crosses the LAS and unemployment returns to its natural level of 6%. If actual inflation falls to 5% but expected inflation remains at 10% unemployment will rise to 8% in the short term due to deflationary pressures and businessmen reducing their demand for labour. Improved levels of long-term efficiency in an economy, i.e. supply side measures, will reduce the long term natural level of unemployment and shift the vertical LAS to, for example 4% as indicated as capacity and employment levels increase.

Multiple Choice

Aggregate Demand and Supply

1. In the diagram below, AD represents the aggregate demand curve, AS represents the aggregate supply curve and Y1 is the current equilibrium level of real income.

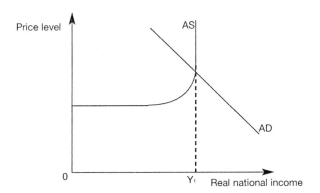

In this situation a reflationary economic policy would cause

a. an increase in both real output and the price level

b. a decrease in both real output and the price level

c. an increase in the price level only

d. an increase in the real output only

e. a decrease in the price level only

f. none of the above.

2. A shift in an economy's aggregate demand curve from AD1 to AD2 as shown in the diagram could have been caused by

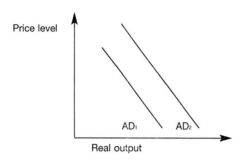

a. a decrease in real interest rates

b. an increase in indirect taxes

c. an increase in labour productivity

d. a decrease in the use of credit cards

e. an increase in the rate of inflation

f. none of the above.

3. If the aggregate supply curve is perfectly elastic, an increase in aggregate demand will lead to

a. a fall in consumption

b. an increase in unemployment

c. an increase in prices

d. an increase in real output

e. a fall in production

f. none of the above.

4. The diagram illustrates an aggregate supply schedule and aggregate demand schedules for an economy. Which of the following statements is/are correct?

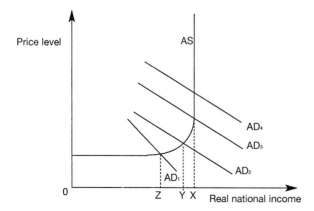

a. The full employment level of real national income is OY.

b. An increase in aggregate demand from AD3 to AD4 could have caused by an increase in savings.

c. An increase in aggregate demand from AD2 to AD3 could have been caused by a fall in investment.

d. The non-accelerating inflation rate of unemployment is OZ.

e. An increase in aggregate demand from AD1 to AD2 would be associated with rises in output and in the price level.

f. None of the above.

5. Supply side measures to promote growth and reduce unemployment might include

a. an increase in protectionist policies

b. a reduction in the rate of value added tax

c. an increase in unemployment benefits

d. pay restraints for public sector employees

e. policies to promote competition

f. raising interest rates.

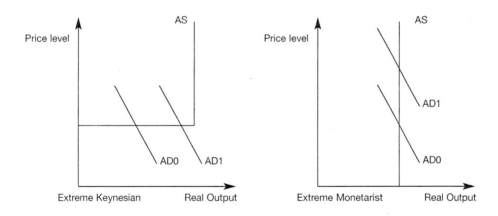

6. Extreme keynesian differ from extreme monetarists because they believe:-

a. real output can always be increased by demand management policies

b. costs are constant for some output levels

c. full employment can be influenced by demand policies

d. none of the above.

Index

Printed in the United Kingdom
by Lightning Source UK Ltd.
2857